tland

AA

M I N I G U I D E

CW00322695

ACHRAY FOREST

Authors: Ann F Stonehouse, John Baxter, David Winpenny and Pat and Charles Aithie
Verifier: Ann F Stonehouse
Managing Editor: Paul Mitchell
Art Editor: Alison Fenton
Editor: Sandy Draper
Cartography provided by the Mapping Services Department of AA Publishing
Internal colour reproduction: Matt Swann

Produced by AA Publishing
© Automobile Association Developments Limited 2007

  This product includes mapping data licensed from the Ordnance Survey® with the permission of the Controller of Her Majesty's Stationery Office. © Crown copyright 2007. All rights reserved. Licence number 100021153.

A03033

TRADE ISBN-13. 978-0-7495-5588-7
SPECIAL ISBN-13: 978-0-7495-5695-2

A CIP catalogue record for this book is available from the British Library.

The contents of this book are believed correct at the time of printing. Nevertheless, the publishers cannot be held responsible for any errors or omissions or for changes in the details given in this book or for the consequences of any reliance on the information it provides. We have tried to ensure accuracy in this book, but things do change and we would be grateful if readers would advise us of any inaccuracies they may encounter. This does not affect your statutory rights.

Visit AA Publishing's website www.theAA.com/travel

Colour reproduction by Keene Group, Andover.
Printed in China by Everbest.

HIGHLAND CATTLE

EDINBURGH

CONTENTS

INTRODUCTION 8

EDINBURGH & FIFE 26

TROSSACHS & SOUTHERN HIGHLANDS 58

ARGYLL, MULL & WESTERN HIGHLANDS 98

CAIRNGORMS & CENTRAL HIGHLANDS 154

SKYE & NORTHERN HIGHLANDS 194

useful information 250

index & acknowledgements 252

Scotland is a country of huge spaces and mountains on a grand scale not found anywhere else in Britain. It is a nation steeped in history and cultural diversity, the violent conflicts with its southern neighbour only one strand in its fascinating history. Scotland's western seaboard is littered with islands – some great, some tiny – and with vast fjord-like sea lochs penetrating to the heart of the highest mountains. This is the crucible of what we now think of as the Scottish identity, and yet it is only part of the story. In the southeast the border lands have their own unique identity, their rounded sheep-shaven hilltops and deep valleys producing many tales and a character and a people very different from the swirling Celtic kilts of the west. The southwest too has its own stories, with its Celtic origins mixed up with Britons, Irish and Viking traditions.

PITLOCHRY

As the ideal destination for active holidays, the Scottish Highlands were first 'discovered' at the end of the 18th century, when fear of wilderness and mountains gave way to the Romantic movement that celebrated the majesty and wonder of the natural landscape. Visitors came to gaze in awe and thrill at the major events of recent history that included a doomed Jacobite monarchy and the last gasps of the feudal clan system. By the time Queen Victoria fell in love with it all in the mid-19th century, sporting estates were taking hold, and the country was perceived by some as a limitless playground for the pursuits of hunting, shooting and fishing.

Today, these traditional, monied sports still play an important part in the economy of the Highlands, but most visitors are drawn here for other activities – walking, birding, winter adventure and water-sports, including quad-biking, sea-kayaking, mountaineering, white-water rafting and mountain-biking.

In the 20th century, the introduction of major conservation projects encouraged the survival and even the reintroduction of creatures such as otters, red squirrels, ospreys and white-tailed sea eagles, and this work continues into the 21st century with the designation of two large national parks, covering the beautiful and accessible Trossachs and Loch Lomond area, and the unique environment of the Cairngorm Mountains.

But as any modern visitor will quickly discover, the Highlands are a great deal more than one big adventure playground. There are layers of history to uncover, from prehistoric burial sites and ancient lake dwellings, to castles, battlefields and industrial trails. Scottish hospitality is legendary for its generosity and warmth, and the pleasures of discovering top-class locally produced food such as beef, salmon and seafood, not to mention good whisky, are all part of the essential Scottish experience.

MULL

ESSENTIAL SPOTS

Join the thronging crowds at Edinburgh's fabulous Arts Festival in August...
hear the chilling lament of a lone piper at atmospheric Glen Coe...take a
cable-car to the top of the Nevis range for stunning panoramic views...chug
nostalgically through the Glenfinnan Valley on a Jacobite steam train...slowly
navigate the excellent loch system of the Caledonian Canal...play a round of
golf on the hallowed links of St Andrews...sail around the islands, steeped
in history and mystery, off the west coast of Scotland...follow the intrepid
explorer R F Scott's epic journey to Antarctica on the RRS *Discovery*...visit the
museums and fine art galleries of cultural Glasgow... don your ski gear and
take to the slopes at Aviemore.

1

3 Bidean nam Bian
This is the highest mountain in Argyll (3,765 feet/1148m) and one of the famous Munros, Scottish peaks over 3,000 feet (900m) high.

1 Oban Bay
Evening sunshine bathes Oban in a lovely glow. The port is the start point for ferries to the Inner and Outer Hebrides.

2 Glen Affric
Dog Falls in Glen Affric, a national nature reserve, is popular with walkers. Also, several species of dragonflies breed there.

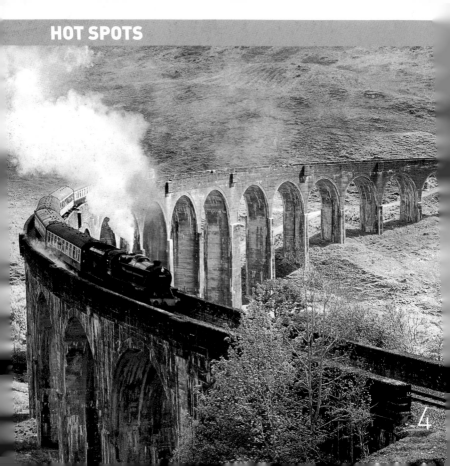

4

5

4 Glenfinnan Viaduct
The 'Hogwarts Express' was filmed crossing the viaduct in the second *Harry Potter* film.

5 Inverary Castle Park
Highland cattle graze in the grounds of this magnificent castle. Several walks allow you to explore the estate on foot.

6 Glasgow
A Charles Rennie Mackintosh design at House for an Art Lover.

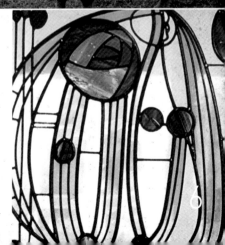

6

Day One in Scotland

For many people a weekend break or a long weekend is a popular way of spending their leisure time. These pages suggest a loosely planned itinerary designed to ensure that you make the most of your time and see and enjoy the very best the area has to offer. Options for wet weather and to entertain children are given where possible.

Friday Night

If your budget will stand it, spend your first night in luxury at The Scotsman, one of the capital's premier hotels, once the headquarters of *The Scotsman* newspaper, and located in the centre of town, close to Waverley Station. Dine in the funky North Bridge Brasserie, or the more formal Vermilion restaurant, before taking a stroll around the city.

Saturday Morning

From the modern Scottish capital, head north across the Forth bridge, passing through the edge of Fife to the ancient capital of Perth. Continue on the fast A9 towards Pitlochry, and turn off to visit the lovely town of Dunkeld. Enjoy a quiet stroll around the 'Little Houses' and the abbey, and perhaps pause for a quick cup of coffee, before returning to the A9. At Ballinluig turn off westwards into the Trossachs on the A827, passing through Aberfeldy and along the northern shore of Loch Tay, under the shadow of Ben Lawers, to the village of Killin.

LOCH FYNE

Saturday Lunch

With several good pubs and cafés, this makes an excellent stop for lunch, and you can walk along to admire the waterfalls by the bridge, called the Falls of Dochart (but beware of traffic).

Saturday Afternoon

Continue west of the A827 and join the A85 as it heads westwards along Glen Dochart until it reaches Crianlarich. Turn south here down Glen Falloch on the A82, which runs parallel for a short distance with the West Highland Way long-distance trail. The routes split once the trail gets beyond Inverarnan. At this point continue down the west shore of Loch Lomond. At Tarbert bear to the right and follow the A83 up over the hill to Arrochar. Follow this route up to the top of the steep pass of Rest and Be Thankful, and enjoy the stunning views back from the car park at the top. Continue around the head of Loch Fyne and treat yourself to a snack at the Loch Fyne Oyster Bar before making your way further on to Inveraray. Cross the old bridge into the town and turn right onto the A819 up Glen Aray. At the top of Loch Awe bear left onto the A85 and follow it into Oban.

Saturday Night

There's a great choice of comfortable B&Bs in Oban – pick one with a view to the island of Kerrera if you can. There are plenty of excellent eating places in this busy little fishing port, or take fresh fish and chips up to McCaig's Folly for a romantic view of the sunset.

Day Two in Scotland

Our second and final day starts with a visit to the Sea Life Sanctuary near Barcaldine or a trip to Glen Coe, before driving north through beautiful countryside to Fort William and then on to the 'big scenery' of lochs and mountains and the romantic Eilean Donan. End the weekend on the lovely island of Skye or, alternatively, drive on to the Highland city of Inverness looking out for Scotland's elusive monster of the deep on the way.

Sunday Morning

After a leisurely breakfast, head north on the A85 and turn off to cross the neck of Loch Etive on the Connel Bridge, on the A828. Visit the doe-eyed seals and many other creatures at the Sea Life Sanctuary south of Barcaldine, or go to the loch-divided village of Ballachulish to explore Glen Coe on the A82.

Sunday Lunch

Continue travelling north on the A82 to Fort William, and turn left on the A830 to stop for lunch at the pub by Neptune's Staircase, the lock staircase by Banavie, at the foot of the Caledonian Canal.

LOCH NESS

CUILLIN HILLS

Sunday Afternoon and Night

Return to the A82 and turn north, following the road up the Great Glen, along the flank of Loch Lochy. Here you can choose to head west on the A87 towards Skye, or continue northeast to Inverness. If taking the first option, the road leads through dramatic mountains to Loch Duich and the famously picturesque castle of Eilean Donan. You can get a cup of tea and a snack here, before continuing to Kyle of Lochalsh, where the modern road bridge will take you to Skye in the twinkling of an eye. Visit the Brightwater Visitor Centre at Kyleakin village for an insight into the local wildlife, before continuing your exploration of the island. There's plenty of top-notch accommodation and eating places, including the elegant Three Chimneys in the north at Colbost (advance booking is essential).

Alternatively, and for a shorter route, stay on the A82 at Invergarry and you'll soon reach the foot of mysterious and atmospheric Loch Ness. The road runs up the western shore, and at Drumnadrochit you can chase the tall tales and sightings of the Loch Ness Monster. The A831 leads off from here towards Cannich and lovely Glen Affric – perfect for a good walk. Stay on the A82 to reach Inverness, a hub of modern communications and full of hotels and B&Bs. Treat yourself to fine dining amid the ancestral portraits at the Bunchrew House Hotel and spend the night in a luxurious room overlooking Beauly Firth (and keep a watchful eye open for the hotel's ghost as you retire to bed!).

STIRLING

Edinburgh & Fife

EAST NEUK VILLAGES

EDINBURGH

ST ANDREWS & FIFE

STIRLING

Edinburgh, Scotland's
gracious capital city, a rich
mix of confident modern
style overlaying 18th-century
elegance and ancient history,
is the popular gateway for
visitors planning to explore
the Highlands. Its outstanding
museums provide the
context for key events and
personalities throughout
Scottish history, while its
thriving arts and commercial
scene showcases the best in
new Scottish talent. Within
easy reach of the city are the
miniature delights of Fife,
including the famous golf
course at St Andrews.

EDINBURGH

Unmissable attractions

Skirt the southeastern coastline visiting the picturesque little fishing villages of East Neuk, with their neat rows of brightly coloured houses and industrious old fishing quays...spend some time in elegant Edinburgh, the jewel of this area's crown, dominated by its magnificent brooding castle high up on a basalt rock hill, and stay to enjoy the world-famous Edinburgh arts festival...or just enjoy fantastic shopping and some great places to eat and drink...don some warm outdoor gear and take to the rugged mass of Arthur's Seat on foot or on a mountain bike...imagine the scenes of carnage at the battlefield of Bannockburn, where, in the 14th century, hero Robert the Bruce and his troops took on Scotland's old adversary the English and won...play a leisurely round on one of the hallowed greens at St Andrews.

1

1 Hillend Ski Centre
Here you can ski or board on the longest artificial slope in Britain.

2 Stirling
The city has stunning Stirling Castle and the Wallace Monument.

3 Pittenweem
This traditional red-roofed fishing village has reinvented itself as a centre for artists.

4

4 St Andrews
A long of golden sandy beach and world-class golf draw visitors here.

5 Arthur's Seat
Edinburgh's residents jog, walk and cycle on this hill near the city centre.

EAST NEUK VILLAGES

A 'fringe of gold' is how James II described the coastal villages of this eastern corner (and 'neuk' is a Scots word for corner) of Fife, way back in the 15th century. However, he was referring to the area's many prosperous little fishing communities rather than golden stretch of beaches, although these can be found too, at Elie and around Largo Bay.

Most of this shoreline is rocky, and the villages that cluster around their diminutive harbours seem to be packed in as tightly as sardines huddled against the rising land. They are characterised by neat little harbours piled high with lobster pots and fishing nets, buildings with pantile roofs and whitewashed, crow step gables, thick stone walls and small windows to fend off the elements – little fisher houses clustered along winding narrow lanes that grew up long before motorised vehicles were dreamed of. In fact, you could drive through Fife on the A917 and overlook these little gems completely, but approach from the sea or on foot along the route of the Fife Coastal Path and it is a different matter.

The East Neuk villages are strung out in line: Elie, St Monans, Pittenweem, Anstruther and Crail. Each has its own character. Picturesque Pittenweem, for instance, was the main fisheries port for the area, and had a priory in the 13th century which was dedicated to Fillan, a 7th-century saint who lived in a cave and converted the local Picts to Christianity.

Anstruther was a major herring port and has the feel of a resort town, with seafront shops selling sweets and fish and chips. It also has a darker side, as an historic centre for smuggling. A chief attraction today is the Scottish Fisheries Museum, an extensive and fascinating collection of fishing craft and stories down the ages. St Monan's, dominated by the squat tower of its 14th-century Auld Kirk,

ANSTRUTHER

EDINBURGH

was noted for ship-building as well as fishing in the 19th century.

Elie, with its golden sands, became a popular seaside holiday resort in the 19th century. A causeway leads to a rocky islet, with panoramic views across the Firth of Forth, and a watersports centre. And Crail, the most easterly of the villages, had particularly strong trading links with the Low Countries, which is reflected in its architecture and in the tolbooth bell, which came from Holland in 1520.

EDINBURGH

Edinburgh grew up in medieval times as a warren of narrow streets around the ancient castle. Wealth led to expansion in the 18th century and the gracious development of the New Town. Today it is the grand home of the new Scottish Parliament, and is the financial, legal and tourism hub of Scotland. Its annual arts festivals are world renowned, and in 2005 the city was declared the first ever literary capital

Visit

ROYAL BOTANIC GARDEN

The largest collection of Chinese plants to be found outside China grows in the Royal Botanic Garden in Edinburgh. The Chinese Hillside is just one of the many delights to be explored in this beautiful, green oasis, which has 5,000 plants in the rockery garden alone. The gardens cover 70 acres (28ha) of landscaped and wooded grounds in the north of the city and hide an art gallery, a café and shop.

of Europe because of its numerous connections with esteemed writers over the centuries, from Sir Walter Scott, Robert Louis Stevenson and Arthur Conan Doyle to modern writers including the children's author, J K Rowling, and Alexander McCall Smith.

Central Edinburgh is relatively compact, and divides into two halves: the narrow, steep, curving streets of the Old Town to the south of Princes Street Gardens, and the neat grid-

EDINBURGH

patterned, broad boulevards and crescents of the New Town to the north of Princes Street.

The Old Town is built along a ridge of rock that stretches from the castle for around a mile eastwards to Holyrood Palace, which lies in the shadow of the tilted volcanic hill of Arthur's Seat. All the main streets run parallel to this line – Queen Street, George Street (great for designer shopping) and Princes Street (good high street shopping) to the north; Castle Street, Lawnmarket, High Street and Canongate (which together form the famous 'Royal Mile') run along the top of the ridge; and Grassmarket, Cowgate and Chambers Street (home to the Royal Museum and Museum of Scotland) less regularly to the south.

The best places to get your bearings are from the top of Calton Hill, at the east end of Princes Street, or standing at the castle esplanade. Views extend north to the Firth of Forth, the Forth bridges and the hills of central Scotland, south to the Pentland Hills, and east to the conical mound of Berwick Law.

The main highlight of the Old Town is magnificent Edinburgh Castle, a solid symbol of the Scottish nation which has withstood centuries of battering. It was mostly destroyed during the Lang Siege of 1567–1573, but was rebuilt by James Douglas, Earl of Morton, regent to the young James VI. Edinburgh's role in modern times as a garrison fortress is celebrated each summer with a military tattoo, with regimental displays and pipe bands from places around the world. The greatest treasures on display here are the royal crown and sceptre, with the Stone of Destiny, on which Scottish kings were once crowned.

The Museum of Scotland is housed in a strikingly modern building in the Old Town. This is where you can see Scottish treasures including the famous Lewis chess pieces, the exquisite 1st-century Hunterston brooch and

EDINBURGH

Insight

UNDERGROUND EDINBURGH

Edinburgh's Old Town is thickly piled – upon itself. For an atmospheric and rather creepy insight into the living conditions here in the mid-18th century, you can visit Mary King's Close, a narrow alleyway opposite St Giles Cathedral, preserved when the City Chambers were built straight over the top. More of these buried streets riddle the foundations of the Old Town, and can be seen in the Tron Kirk, on the Royal Mile.

Visit

GREYFRIAR'S BOBBY

Edinburgh's favourite statue is much less imposing than the Scott Monument on Princes Street, and stands at the top of Candlemaker Row, opposite the Museum of Scotland. It depicts a Skye terrier, and was raised in 1873 in memory of a little dog who slept faithfully on his master's grave in the nearby Greyfriars Kirkyard for 14 years after the man's death, fed on scraps from local sympathisers.

the beautiful 8th-century Monymusk Reliquary. The comprehensive collections at this fine museum help to explain Scottish history from its earliest times to the present.

Edinburgh's so-called New Town covers an area of about 1 square mile (318ha) to the north of Princes Street, and is characterised by broad streets of spacious terraced houses with large windows and ornamental door arches. Until the mid-18th century, Edinburgh had been neatly contained on the ridge between Arthur's Seat and the castle. Conditions became overcrowded and insanitary and, as a new age of scientific advance and intellectual enlightenment dawned, so the need for expansion became clear. A competition was held in 1766 to design a new city to the north. The winner was unknown architect James Craig (1744–1795), and within three years the first house was ready. The first New Town was so successful that a second one was laid out in 1802, extending north towards Leith. While Princes Street has lost its shine in the glare of modern commerce, the broad Charlotte Square, with its preserved Georgian House, is the epitome of the planners' intentions.

The North Bridge was needed to enable pedestrians to reach the new city without foundering in the (then) muddy valley. A second link, the Mound, came about by accident, when 'Geordie' Boyd, a clothier in the Old Town, started to dump earth rubble in the marsh. Soon the builders from the New Town joined in, as they dug out foundations for the new buildings and dumped the residue. It took two million cartloads of rubble to complete the job, and the causeway became the Mound, later home to the National Gallery. This superb collection of paintings includes works by talented Scottish painters such as Henry Raeburn, Allen Ramsay, David Wilkie and William McTaggart, in addition to the masters, Vermeer, Van Dyke, Raphael and Monet.

The tour buses that congregate on Waverley Bridge, by the main railway station, offer the easiest and most efficient introduction to the city, with a choice of four different routes taking in the main attractions and linking you to the sites outside the city centre such as the Botanical Gardens and the old port of Leith (good for shopping, trendy bars and the Royal Yacht Britannia).

ST ANDREWS & FIFE

St Andrews is famous for two things – as the home of golf and of an ancient university. The broad sweeps of irresistible golden sands that lie to the north of St Andrews attracted the attention of Adolf Hitler during World War II, who saw them as the perfect landing site for a planned invasion force. Although his plans came to nothing concrete anti-tank defences may still be glimpsed along the tree line.

The undulating lush turf between the beaches and the more fertile farmland is known in Scotland as the links, a term which has become almost synonymous with golf courses. St Andrews is where

Visit

NUCLEAR SECRETS

A hole, 131 feet (40m) deep, in the ground between St Andrews and Anstruther was the secret location of Scotland's Nuclear Command Centre, built in the 1950s as fear of the Cold War was growing. It is eerie to think that, in the event of nuclear attack, a self-supporting military community of around 300 people could have survived in the cramped conditions of this concrete-lined shelter. In 1994 the bunker opened its doors to the public as Scotland's Secret Bunker

Street, South Street and Market Street the main arteries spreading west from the cathedral. Before the building's destruction during the Reformation in the 16th century, this was known as the ecclesiastical heart of Scotland, and a major pilgrimage site. The castle in its present form dates from around 1390, but was originally constructed by the bishops as essential defence. Its most remarkable features lie underground: the chilling bottle dungeon, 24 feet (7.3m) deep and hewn from solid rock under a tower, from which no prisoner could escape. A mine and counter mine are legacies of an attempt to break a siege of 1546–1547 by the Duke of Argyll. His men tunnelled towards the castle but were thwarted when the defenders dug out a counter-mine and headed them off.

the 18-hole game is said to have originated in 1764, and has six of them, of which the Old Course of the fine Royal and Ancient Golf Club, founded in 1754, is the most famous.

The town itself received its royal charter in the mid-12th century, and the spectacular ruined cathedral above the harbour dates from then. St Andrews retains its medieval street plan, with North

Today, what might have become simply an elegant and sleepy resort town is kept wide awake by its thriving university – Scotland's most venerable – which dates from 1413.

STIRLING CASTLE

The National Trust for Scotland owns two contrasting properties on this eastern tip of Fife, which both show the hand of the master Arts and Crafts restorer, Robert Lorimer (1864–1929). In the rolling hills to the south of the bustling town of Cupar lies the Hill of Tarvit Mansionhouse, an Edwardian house filled with elegant furniture and fine paintings, and surrounded by formal gardens. In contrast, by a peaceful corner to the south, just inland from St Monans, lies beautiful Kellie Castle, dating from 1360, and restored with eccentric charm by the Lorimer family. The castle is set beside an interesting, rambling, walled Arts and Crafts garden.

STIRLING

This ancient royal burgh grew up around a strategic crossing point of the River Forth before it widens to the east and becomes impassable. The Old Bridge, at the northern end of the town, carried the only route northwards on this side of the country, and Stirling remained the key to the north until the Kincardine Bridge opened to the southeast in 1936. Plans for a second bridge are under way.

The town's most spectacular landmark is its castle, set high above the once-marshy plain on a rocky crag, and fought over by Scots and English in the 13th and 14th centuries. It was later remodelled as a royal palace favoured by Stuart kings, becoming the birthplace of James II and James IV, temporary home to an infant Mary, Queen of Scots, and the chosen site of James VI's coronation. Visitors can tour the castle with its re-created kitchens and see the exhibition in the Queen Anne casemates. In the Chapel Royal there are two tapestries that represent a modern reworking of the Hunt of the Unicorn series.

Fabulous views from the castle's Esplanade extend to the Campsie Fells in the west and the start of the Highland hills to the north. Several magnificent 17th-century buildings

49

Visit

FRUITFUL FOLLY

Southeast of Stirling, near the village of Dunmore, sits a distinctive folly, a rare example of architecture inspired by fruit. It's the Pineapple, a garden retreat built to adorn Dunmore Park in 1761 by John Murray, the 4th Earl. The rendered stone foliage tops an octagonal Gothic tower. Nobody knows quite why it was built, but pineapples were considered a rare and exotic delicacy at the time. The attractive gardens and surrounding parkland are owned by the National Trust for Scotland, and the Landmark Trust lets out the folly as holiday accommodation.

can be seen in the old town, including Argyll's Lodging (once used as a military hospital), before Victorian developments take over at the bottom of the hill.

Stirling's other great landmark is the National Wallace Monument, the tower which crowns Abbey Craig. It was built in a revival of nationalist sentiment in 1869, to commemorate the Battle of Stirling Bridge in 1297, when William Wallace won a victory against Edward I's English forces, killing thousands and hounding the wounded into the marshes to die. The structure now houses this patriotic hero's broadsword, and you can climb the 246 steps to the top for views to the distant Forth Bridges.

Just to the south of Stirling, the battlefield of Bannockburn was the site of a major Scots victory in their wars against English oppression in 1314. King Robert the Bruce took on the superior forces of Edward II and won decisively. Stirling was the last English stronghold north of the River Forth, and while its fall was only a stage in the fight for independence (which would continue to rage on for another 14 years), this great victory consolidated the power of Robert I, effectively silencing any rival claimants to the Scottish throne. For the first time, the Scots were able to present a united front against their old enemy.

PLACES OF INTEREST

Aquarium
The Scores, St Andrews.
Tel: 01334 474786;
www.standrewsaquarium.co.uk

Argyll's Lodging
Castle Wynd, Old Town, Stirling.
Tel: 01786 431319;
www.historicscotland.gov.uk

Bannockburn Visitor Centre
Glasgow Road, Stirling.
Tel: 01786 812664

British Golf Museum
Bruce Embankment, St Andrews.
Tel: 01334 460046;
www.britishgolfmuseum.co.uk

Crail Museum and Heritage Centre
62–64 Markgate, Crail.
Tel: 01333 450869

Edinburgh Castle
Tel: 0131 225 9846;
www.historic-scotland.gov/uk

Georgian House
Charlotte Square, Edinburgh.
Tel: 0131 226 3318

Hill of Tarvit Mansionhouse
2 miles/3.2km south of Cupar off A916.
Tel: 01334 653127

Isle of May/May Princess
Kiosk at Anstruther Harbour.
Tel: 01333 310103;
www.isleofmayferry.com

Kellie Castle (NTS)
Northwest of Pittenweem.
Tel: 01333 720271

Museum of Scotland
Chambers Steet, Edinburgh.
Tel: 0131 247 4422; www.nms.ac.uk

National Gallery of Scotland
The Mound, Edinburgh.
Tel: 0131 624 6200;
www.nationalgalleries.org

National Wallace Monument
Abbey Craig, Stirling.
Tel: 01786 472140;
www.nationalwallacemonument.com

The Pineapple
Dunmore Park, Dunmore.
Tel: 01324 831137

Real Mary King's Close
2 Warriston's Close, High Street,
Edinburgh. Tel: 08702 430160;
www.realmarykingsclose.com

Royal Botanic Garden
Inverleith Row, Edinburgh.
Tel: 0131 552 7171; www.rbge.org.uk

Scottish Fisheries Museum
Harbourhead, Anstruther.
Tel: 01333 310628;
www.scotfishmuseum.org
St Andrews Cathedral and Castle
South Street, St Andrews.
Tel: 01334 477196
Stirling Castle
Upper Castle Hill, Stirling.
Tel: 01786 450000;
www.historic-scotland.gov/uk

FOR CHILDREN
Blair Drummond Safari Park
Blair Drummond, by Stirling.
Tel: 01786 841456;
www.blairdrummond.com
Old Town Jail
St John Street, Stirling.
Tel: 01786 450050;
www.oldtownjail.com
Scotland's Secret Bunker
Crown Buildings, Troywood,
near St Andrews.
Tel: 01333 310301
Scottish Deer Centre
Bow-of-Fife, by Cupar.
Tel:01337 810391; www.tsdc.co.uk

SHOPPING
In Edinburgh, George Street,
Victoria Street, Harvey Nichols on
St Andrew Square

SPORTS & ACTIVITIES
COASTAL PATH
Fife Coastal Path. Forth Bridge to
Tay Bridge, 81 miles (122km).
CYCLE HIRE
Biketrax
Tollcross, Edinburgh.
Tel: 0131 228 6633
ADVENTURE SPORTS
East Neuk Outdoors
Cellardyke Park, Anstruther.
Tel: 01333 311929
Cluny Clays
Cluny Mains Farm, by Kirkcaldy.
Tel: 01592 720374

ANNUAL EVENTS & CUSTOMS
Edinburgh
International Festival and Fringe
Festival, Aug.
Military Tattoo, Aug.
Hogmanay, 31 Dec.

53

George Inter-Continental

19–21 George Street,
Edinburgh, EH2 2PB
Tel: 0131 225 1251

Afternoon tea is celebrated in refined elegance at this gracious New Town hotel, designed by Robert Adam. Pass through the marble-floored foyer and look up at the detailed plasterwork and fine chandeliers. The lobby lounge serves tea and snacks throughout the day. Choose from a traditional Highland tea, served from 3pm, with finger sandwiches and Dundee cake, or Georgian tea with champagne and millionaire's shortbread, or perhaps dip into gravadlax and Belgian waffles from the à la carte menu.

Kind Kyttock's Kitchen

Cross Wynd, Falkland, KY15 7BE

If you're exploring in Fife, let the aroma of freshly baked scones and pancakes entice you to this comfortable, well-established tea room in the historic village of Falkland. The preserves and cakes are home-made, too, and a small selection is offered for sale. Soups, sandwiches, salads and sweets are also served at lunchtime.

The Tea Room

158 Canongate, Royal Mile,
Edinburgh, EH8 8DD
Tel: 07771 501679
www.the-tea-room.info

This charming tea room is decorated with beautiful linen tablecloths and watercolours by local artists, and opens its doors daily for light lunches and delicious teas. Choose a traditional afternoon tea, or treat yourself to a cream tea, with home-baked scones and cakes. Come on a Thursday afternoon to have your tea leaves read.

GLEN FALLOCH

CRAIL

Cross Keys Hotel
Main Street, Kippen, FK8 3DN
Tel: 01786 870293

Kippen is a small village in the Fintry Hills, some 10 miles (16km) west of Stirling and just off the A811. Close by, lovely Burnside Wood is managed by people from a local community group, and is perfect for walking and nature trails. This friendly pub, dating from 1703, on the high street offers excellent home-made food, including a creamy smoked haddock omelette, and steak and mushroom pie. Beers include Harviestoun Bitter & Twisted. Children are welcome, and dogs are allowed too.

Doric Tavern
15–16 Market Street,
Edinburgh, EH1 1DE
Tel: 0131 225 1084
www.thedoric.co.uk

A good public bar, bistro and wine bar offer something for everybody in this comfortable and authentic popular Old Town hostelry, a short way from the castle. There is a full range of seafood, game, meat and vegetarian dishes on the bistro menu, including Scottish old favourites such as Cullen skink and haggis. More traditional pub food is on offer downstairs in the Doric Bar.

The Ship Inn
The Toft, Elie, KY9 1DT
Tel: 01333 330246

Elie is a perfect place to stop in the East Neuk villages. On the busy waterfront at Elie Bay, The Ship has been here since 1838. Activities such as beach cricket, live music and summer Sunday barbecues all add to the friendly, relaxed atmosphere. The full menu makes the most of good local suppliers, including fish from St Monans and haggis from nearby Lundin Links. The wide range of beers include Bellhaven Best, and the wine list is extensive and eclectic. Children and dogs are both made welcome here.

KINNOULL HILL

Trossachs &
Southern Highlands

ABERFELDY

CALLANDER

CRIEFF

DUNDEE

DUNKELD

KILLIN

KIRRIEMUIR

PERTH

PITLOCHRY

TROSSACHS NATIONAL PARK

INTRODUCTION

This central belt of Scotland offers hills and mountains, silvery rivers and lochs, with some of the best golf courses in the country. It is a place of dense woodland and fertile farmland, dotted with humble fishing villages and grand mansions, ultra-modern engineering projects and ancient battlefields. Popular with tourists and walkers since the mid-19th century, it has also become the centre of the recent growth of adrenalin sports in Scotland, with opportunities for taking to the water in kayaks, canoes, rafts, and on bodyboards and windsurfers. Abseiling and hill walking are also popular here.

Unmissable attractions

Feel the adrenalin rush as you go white-water rafting on the River Tay at Perth...admire the Victorian architecture of Callander, the eastern gateway to the rugged Trossachs...venture below decks on the wooden RRS *Discovery* and see how Captain Scott and his crew lived on their daring exploration to Antarctica...sample the best of Scottish whisky at one of the area's many distilleries...visit the Scottish Crannog Centre where you can see restored Iron Age dwellings and craftsmen demonstrating crafts of days gone by... witness magnificent ospreys in the nest or circling high above near Dunkeld... enjoy the breathtaking view of the dramatic and beautiful Glen Lyon.

1

2 The Hermitage, Dunkeld
This is a grove of giant trees by the rapids and waterfalls of the River Braan in Perthshire.

3 Edzell Castle
The castle is partly in ruins, but enough remains for an enjoyable visit, and its summer house is intact. The real glory here is the walled garden.

1 The Knock, Crieff
The town of Crieff sits on Knock Hill, although the summit is outside the town. The views across the countryside are simply magnificent.

4

4 RRS *Discovery*
Sailor, Robert Falcon Scott's successful Royal Navy career saw him promoted to the rank of Commander in the same month he became leader of an Antarctic expedition aboard *Discovery*. Scott wrote about the 1901–04 journey in the book *The Voyage of the Discovery*, published in 1905.

5 Cycling near Crieff
Cycling in Perthshire is as popular as ever, with challenging routes through the hilly country.

6 Aberfeldy
Canoeing on a quiet stretch of water at Loch Tay near Aberfeldy. White-water rafting is also popular in the area along with waterskiing.

ABERFELDY

Born in Ireland, General George Wade (1673–1748) served as Commander-in-Chief of North Britain from 1724–40, and left his lasting mark on the Highlands in the form of almost 250 miles (400km) of military roads and some 40 bridges to go with them. Today, one of his finest bridges still carries the traffic of the A827 over the River Tay at Aberfeldy, a pleasant stone-built town in the heart of Perthshire. The bridge's elegant structure, with its four obelisks and five graceful spans, was designed for Wade by the architect William Adam. On the bank near by stands a monument to the Black Watch Regiment.

Signs in the town point the way to walking trails that lead to the Birks of Aberfeldy, birchwoods celebrated by the poet Robert Burns. The town's historic watermill is now the setting for a good bookshop, gallery, music shop and café. On the edge of the town, the Dewar's distillery offers a visitor centre

Insight

PONTIUS PILATE

The pretty hamlet of Fortingall, at the entrance to Glen Lyon, is claimed by some to be the birthplace of Pontius Pilate. It is said that he was born here, the son of a Roman soldier and a local girl, before rising to become the Roman prefect of Judea and Samaria. His most notorious act was to condemn Christ to crucifixion, and tales of his ultimate fate are obscure – did he really convert to Christianity and live to a ripe old age in Switzerland? The Fortingall connection seems to have arisen from a mysterious headstone in the churchyard, marked simply 'PP'.

and tour, culminating in a tasting. Outside you might see native red squirrels. To the west, at Weem, is the 16th-century stronghold of Castle Menzies, a restored Z-plan tower house. One of the rooms used by Bonnie Prince Charlie has been furnished and decorated in the style he would have known.

67

Loch Tay lies 5 miles (8km) to the west of Aberfeldy, with the picturesque village of Kenmore at its eastern end. A splendidly spired gateway marks an entrance to Taymouth Castle, now a popular golfing holiday resort. The town also has a great watersports centre, but its most unusual attraction is a replica round-house or crannog, set low over the waters of the loch. This is part of the Scottish Crannog Centre, the visitor centre for an on-going project that is exploring and excavating the 18 or so similar Iron Age dwellings that once lined these attractive shores.

Crannogs were community dwellings built on wooden stilts. The cold, peaty water of the loch has helped to preserve the original timbers, plants and food remains and even scraps of cloth, and the discoveries made here reveal much about the way of life of the crannog builders. Visitors are able to watch demonstrations of ancient crafts and to participate in them.

Shortly before it reaches Aberfeldy, the Tay is joined by the waters of the River Lyon. This river flows down from one of Scotland's most beautiful valleys, Glen Lyon, which lies sandwiched between Loch Tay and Loch Rannoch. Entry to the glen is via the dramatic, steep-sided pass at Fortingall, or over the mountain pass by Ben Lawers.

CALLANDER

Callander straddles the A84 northwest of Stirling, and is the eastern gateway to the Trossachs. During the 19th century it was a flourishing resort town, and the grandeur of the Victorian buildings along its main street bears this out.

On a summer's day the little town is packed out with visitors, keen to enjoy the varied shops and tea rooms, and to track down the history of Rob Roy, a folk hero. Rob Roy MacGregor (1671–1734) took refuge with his people in the local hills, and his story is told at the visitor centre in the former church

CALLANDER

on the main square. His grave is in the churchyard at Balquhidder. There are several good walks from the town centre, leading to Bracklinn Falls and the Callander Crags.

The Hamilton Toy Collection in Main Street has toys from the 19th century, including dolls, teddy bears, model train sets, toy soldiers, books, jigsaws and games. It is as popular with adults eager to relive their childhood days, as with children.

Insight

WHO PAYS THE FERRYMAN?

Until 1535, anybody wishing to cross the River Teith at Doune had to pay a ferryman to be rowed across. One day James Spittal was refused passage when he showed up without any money. Spittal was the wealthy tailor to James IV, and took the slight personally. It is said that, out of spiteful anger, he paid for the building of a bridge here to permanently deprive the ferryman of his living. The bridge is still standing, though it was modified in 1866.

To the west of the town, beyond the woollen weaving mill and display at Kilmahog, is the scenic spot of the Pass of Leny, with the Falls of Leny accessible from the roadside car park. Of interest to cyclists, the Callander to Strathyre Cycleway runs past here too, following the route of the former railway line from Callander up the western shore of Loch Lubnaig towards Killin.

To the southwest of Callander lies the Lake of Menteith, where you can hire a boat and fishing tackle and try casting for rainbow trout. Alternatively, a ferry goes out to the tree-covered island where the romantic ruins of Inchmahome Priory stand. Augustinian monks made it their home in 1238, and the infant Mary, Queen of Scots was hidden here for three weeks in 1547 after the Battle of Pinkie Cleugh before she was smuggled to France.

Southeast of Callander on the A84 lies the rural village of Doune, with a substantial ruined castle at its heart, hidden amid the trees on a curve of the River Teith. Built by the powerful regent of Scotland, Robert Stewart, Duke of Albany, in the late 14th century, it is comparatively simple in construction, with a main block of buildings set within a courtyard and contained by a mighty curtain wall. The fabric of the castle is maintained by Historic Scotland. You can climb to the top of this for panoramic views of the village and the surrounding countryside, and there are lots of little stairways and chambers to explore. Its medieval austerity and imposing stature gave the castle a starring role in the film *Monty Python and the Holy Grail*.

CRIEFF

The old spa town of Crieff lies above the River Earn west of Perth, on the edge of the Highlands. For a time in the 17th century it took the alternative name of Drummond, in honour of local patrons, but the original name was restored in the 18th century, after the town was burned down by Jacobite rebels.

Insight

SHAKEY TOUN

Comrie, to the west of Crieff on the A85, has a secret. It was built directly over the geological fault of the Highland Boundary, and in the 19th century it was known as the earthquake capital of Scotland. Seismologists in the 1830s recorded more than 7,000 tremors, along with strange loud noises and sulphurous smells. No serious damage was reported. As a legacy of this activity, Earthquake House stands to the west of the town. It was originally built as a recording station in 1869. Its interior, restored in the 1980s and with modern equipment set up alongside the original seismographs.

Insight

HIGHLAND KITSCH

In Callander you won't be able to escape the Highland kitsch that is everywhere, but its origins at least are ancient. The word 'clan' comes from the Gaelic word 'clann' meaning 'children' but gradually it came to be used to refer to 'kindred'.

Crieff grew up as a centre for cattle drovers, who passed through here on their way south to England or north to the Highlands. The linen and tanning industries thrived for a while, but were overtaken by the growth of the Lowland factories. Today Crieff is an industrious service town, celebrated for the quality of its schools, and as a main hub for activities including fishing, cycling, and watersports on Loch Earn. There is good walking too, with a signposted trail from the town centre north to Knock Hill.

The Drummonds had their castle 3 miles (4.8km) south of the town, and while the castle itself is still private, the fabulous formal 17th-century garden has been restored to its former state and is open on summer afternoons. The burial chapel of the Drummonds stands beside the Innerpeffray Library, founded in 1691 and remarkable as the second oldest library in Scotland.

To the north of Crieff a narrow road leads up the remote Glen

Insight

THE WORST POET IN THE WORLD

Self-taught poet William McGonagall (1830–1902) retains a special place in Scottish hearts for his notoriously bad verse. A Dundee handloom weaver, McGonagal published his first poetry collection in 1878, to the acclaim of many Edinburgh students. His heartfelt verses on the Tay Bridge disaster of 1879, when the bridge collapsed under a passenger train, are particularly memorable for their naïve sentiment and lack of poetic rhythm. restored in the 1980s and with modern equipment set up alongside the original seisomgraphs, may be viewed through the single display window.

Turret to Loch Turret, passing the scenic beauty spot at the waterfalls of the same name. Begun in 1775, Glenturret Distillery is home to the Famous Grouse Experience, which is very entertaining and offers a glimpse into the serious business of making whisky.

DUNDEE

Dundee was founded on a 19th-century industrial base which was famously reduced to the three 'J's: jam, jute and journalism. Today it is busy reinventing itself as a lively centre for the arts and hands-on science, and celebrating its maritime and industrial heritage. The main focus of rejuvenation has been along the waterfront, where the three-masted Royal Research Ship *Discovery* is now berthed. She was built here in 1900–1901, using expertise developed for the whaling industry, and her maiden voyage was to the Antarctic. In 1902 she became trapped in the pack ice, and survived two timber-crunching winters before breaking free and sailing home. The modern museum alongside tells her story. Nothing beats exploring the ship herself, however, and witnessing the cramped conditions of the brave men who crewed her for years at a time.

Moored near by, the frigate *Unicorn* was built in 1824 and is the oldest British warship afloat. In the same corner is *Sensation: Dundee*, a state-of-the-art celebration of science geared to children, centred on the five senses.

Wool and flax were both woven in Dundee, long before the advent of jute in the early 19th century caused a boom in the town's growth. The plant fibre was imported from India and softened with whale oil before being spun and woven. By the 1870s most Indian mills were undercutting Dundee prices, and the industry had to scale down. It was hit hard again by the post-World War I recession. A fascinating survivor is the Verdant Works, which explains among other things how Dundee developed so quickly, and why more women than men were employed by the profitable jute industry.

D C Thomson (1861–1964), son of a Dundee shipping entrepreneur, founded the newspaper company that still bears his name in 1906. *The Sunday Post* and the *Weekly News* are still produced here, along with many

DUNKELD CATHEDRAL

local papers, but the company's best loved creations were its popular comics for children, the *Beano* and *Dandy*. Statues of the characters Minnie the Minx and Desperate Dan can be seen on the High Street.

DUNKELD

A picturesque little 18th-century town with a tiny Gothic cathedral, Dunkeld lies surrounded by glorious woodland on the banks of the River Tay. Everything here, bar the cathedral, was destroyed by the Jacobites after their 1689 victory at Killiecrankie. When it was rebuilt, terraced cottages were squeezed into a compact centre of just two main streets: Cathedral Street and High Street, with a neat little square, called The Cross. The pleasing uniformity of Dunkeld owes much to this rebuilding by the Dukes of Atholl, and more to the carefully done restoration of around 20 houses by the National Trust for Scotland since the 1950s. The Trust has a shop in the main square, in a

Insight

OSPREY HAVEN

The Loch of the Lowes lies to the east of Dunkeld, and is noted for its breeding ospreys. These mighty birds of prey migrate to this spot from west Africa towards the end of March, and have successfully bred here since 1970. Watch them on the nest, and enjoy the rest of the birdlife from the visitor centre, operated by the Scottish Wildlife Trust.

building distinctive for the iron 'ell' mounted on its exterior. The ell was a unit of measurement equivalent to 37 inches (92.5cm). The graceful stone bridge which links Dunkeld to Inver, much favoured as a subject by painters, was a masterpiece in 1809 of the engineer Thomas Telford.

Dunkeld's ruined cathedral stands in a picturesque, shady setting on the banks of the river, and the crumbled building dates back to the 13th century, although its history as a monastic site goes back to the

6th century. Kenneth MacAlpin, the first king of Scotland, brought St Columba's bones here from Iona in around AD 850, thereby making it an important medieval ecclesiastical centre. The most substantial part left standing today is the choir, which still serves as the parish church. Close by the end of the cathedral furthest from the main entrance, look out for a sign indicating the 'Parent Larch'. This particular tree was imported from Austria in 1738, and became the source of many trees in and around nearby forests, planted up by the Dukes of Atholl between 1738–1830.

There are plenty of good circular signposted walks in the woods around here and along the river bank, with carpets of bluebells in late spring, and red squirrels to look out for – a leaflet from the tourist office gives full details. One walk leads through mixed woodland along the River Braan and up to the folly of the Hermitage, or Ossian's Hall, set above the Black Linn Falls.

Little Dunkeld is the last resting place of the great Scottish fiddler, Neil Gow (1727–1807), who composed many dance tunes and fine airs and was famous throughout Britain for his skill. His violin is on display at Blair Castle.

KILLIN

The village of Killin is set beneath the hills where the River Dochart tumbles over an extensive waterfall and into the western end of Loch Tay. Once home to the MacNabs, it is at the heart of the ancient district of Breadalbane, and has now become a popular walking, fishing and touring centre. The interesting Breadalbane Folklore Centre located in St Fillan's Mill shares its premises with the local tourist office, and offers an intriguing insight into Scottish legends of kelpies, brownies and other mythical creatures. The mill originally powered machines for the weaving of tweed. The ruins of 16th-century Finlarig Castle, a Campbell stronghold, stand at the head of the loch. It has what are said to be the only surviving remains in the country of a beheading pit, reserved for the execution of the gentry.

The National Trust for Scotland is noted for its preservation of some grand castles, but lists some more modest dwellings, too. One of the humblest is along the narrow Glen Lochay Road, just north of Killin. Moirlanich Longhouse is a low, long, 19th-century farmhouse built with a cruck frame . At least three generations of the Robertson family lived here, until the 1960s, and the house has been preserved with a 'hingin' lum' (suspended chimney) and traditional wooden-box beds.

The view from Killin up Loch Tay is dominated by the bulk of Ben Lawers, 1,214m (3,984ft), the highest mountain in the area. It is known for its delicate alpine flora, and with the neighbouring Tarmachan range, is a popular focus for walkers. The area is a national nature reserve, and information is available from the Mountain Visitor Centre.

Visit

STORIES IN STONE

Stones and cross-slabs carved in Pictish times are a feature of the landscape over to the west and south of Kirriemuir. Some of the best have been gathered together in the former schoolhouse at Meigle, where they form a fascinating collection dating from the 8th to the 10th centuries. Along with favourite subjects such as salmon, dogs and horsemen, there are stranger creatures to discover, such as birds with bulbous eyes.

KIRRIEMUIR

Kirriemuir is the gateway to the great Glens of Angus, the long valleys which stretch north into the open moorland of the Grampian Mountains, forming the southern edge of the mighty Cairngorms National Park. The range includes Glen Esk, Glen Clova and Glen Prosen, and they all offer superb hill-walking, with Glen Clova giving access to remote Glen Doll. The glens are all home to red and black grouse, golden eagles, ptarmigans and capercaillies, red and roe deer. Antarctic explorer Robert Falcon Scott and Edward Wilson, the expedition's doctor and artist, came to the area to plan their ill-fated voyage to the South Pole, and are commemorated by a memorial fountain in Glen Prosen.

Kirriemuir itself is an industrious red sandstone town, built on the revenues of weaving and farming. The town hosts an annual walking festival in June, and has a small aviation museum, but its main claim to fame is its associations with the playwright and novelist J M Barrie. The creator of Peter Pan was born here in 1860, the son of a weaver and one of ten children, and his birthplace is now an evocative museum. The wash-house round the back of the property served as Barrie's first theatre, and may have inspired the Wendy House in *Peter Pan* (1904). Although he lived for most of his life in London, Barrie wrote with great affection about the small-town life of Kirriemuir, disguised as 'Thrums' in his tales. In 1930 Barrie presented the community with a novel gift after they had honoured him with the freedom of the town: a camera obscura on nearby Kirrie Hill, for far-reaching views over the surrounding countryside (check at the birthplace for opening times).

About 5 miles (8km) to the south of Kirriemuir lies Glamis Castle, family seat of the Earls of Strathmore and Kinghorne, and the childhood home of the late Queen Elizabeth, the Queen Mother. With its multiple turrets and fairy-tale battlements Glamis Castle (pronounced 'Glahms') is a vision of what a Scottish castle should look like, and the interior is equally fabulous too, with moulded plaster ceilings and fine panelling. At its core is a medieval tower house, dating back to around 1372. The surrounding parkland is well worth exploring, with its formal Italian

FALLS OF DOCHART, KILLIN

garden and a pinetum. For a total contrast, six 18th-century cottages in the nearby village house the Angus Folk Museum, showing how the rural community lived.

PERTH

The Roman settlement of Perth was founded on the banks of the River Tay in the 1st century; in the Middle Ages it became the capital of Scotland. Today it is a lively city at the centre of a thriving and established farming community, its compact core offering great shopping and bohemian cafés that spill out onto the pavements. Open-top bus tours from the railway station are a good way to gain an overview. With its theatre, City Hall, a brand new concert hall and other venues, not to mention galleries and cinemas, Perth is an active centre for music and the arts, culminating in a lively festival in May.

Perth's extensive parks are headed by the North Inch and the South Inch, beside the river, and there are several gardens to explore in the area, including Branklyn, which is specially noted for its blue Himalayan poppies (Meconopsis). Scotland's National Heather Collection resides at Bells Cherrybank Gardens, to the west of the city centre, where there are around 900 varieties.

In recent years Perth has developed as the adventure capital of Scotland, with an ever-longer list of adventure sports and activities to take you out and about across the region. So if the more traditional sports of fishing, golf, pony trekking, mountain biking and hill-hiking seem tame, you can get your adrenalin rush by quad biking, off-road driving, abseiling, canoeing, waterskiing, cliff-jumping, white-water rafting or even paintballing – and that's just for a start. The tourist office has more details.

Scone Palace is on the outskirts of the city, a privately owned mansion rich in history. It remains the family seat of the

Earls of Mansfield, and the ancient crowning place of Scottish kings since Robert the Bruce. Forty two kings were crowned on the Stone of Scone – unfortunately the original block is held for safekeeping in Edinburgh Castle, so what you see here is a replica. There are fine bed hangings in the house, which were embroidered by Mary, Queen of Scots herself. The gardens and grounds are attractively planted, and a modern addition is the beech maze, planted in a suitably Scottish tartan pattern.

PITLOCHRY

This bustling town in the wooded valley of the River Tummel is based around one long and very attractive main street, running parallel with the river, and lined with shops and eating places. The geographical heart of Scotland, it first appeared on the map when General Wade built a military road through here, and it has been a popular holiday resort since the 19th century.

A footbridge leads across the river to the Festival Theatre, with its Explorers' Garden, opened in 2003 to celebrate 300 years of botanical exploration and collection of artefacts from around the world by Scots. There is a view from the footbridge to the salmon ladder, which was installed as part of a hydroelectric dam system along the river and which also created Loch Faskally, a local beauty spot. Learn more at the Scottish Hydroelectric Visitor Centre, which gives access to an observation window where you can watch the wild salmon jumping (usually between April and October). Pitlochry boasts two distilleries, both welcome visitors: Bell's Blair Atholl Distillery in the town centre, and tiny Edradour on the outskirts.

Just to the north of the town is the conservation village of Moulin, with its 17th century church and ruined castle in the shadow of Ben Vrackie. The writer Robert Louis Stevenson stayed here in 1881, and described it as a 'sweet spot'.

LOCH KATRINE

Insight

CLAYMORE VERSUS MUSKET

In 1689 John Claverhouse, 'Bonnie Dundee', nicknamed 'Bluidy Clavers' in his persecution of the Covenanters, raised a small army of Highlanders in support of King James II. The Scottish Parliament (the Estates) sent a larger army north under General Hugh Mackay to sort things out. The battle took place on open ground to the north of the Pass of Killiecrankie and it was the last time the claymore conquered the musket in open ground. Some 900 of the 2,500 Highlanders were shot down as they charged, but then the troops had to stop to fix bayonets, which plugged into the muzzle of their muskets. By the time the Highlanders were upon them, they broke and fled. The battle had lasted just three minutes. Half of Mackay's army was killed, captured or drowned in the Garry. Dundee died in battle. A month later his army was defeated at Dunkeld, and 25 years later, when the Highlanders next brought their claymores south for the Stuarts, the troops fixed their bayonets so they didn't block the barrel.

Some three miles (4.8km) north of Pitlochry is the narrow, wooded gorge of Killiecrankie, on the River Garry. This was the site of a battle in 1689 when a Jacobite army defeated government troops. There is a scenic walk of about a mile (1.6km) here.

Continue north and you'll reach Blair Castle, a white-painted mansion in a majestic setting of trees and gardens, with hills behind. It claims to be the most visited hostoric house in Scotland, with Queen Victoria and Robert the Bruce among its guesst. It's been the ancestral home of the Dukes and Earls of Atholl for more than 700 years, and can claim its own private army. The castle itself is located on the main route north through the Highlands which made it a strategic prize in several major conflicts. Bonnie Prince Charlie slept in the little, now tartan-clad tower room in 1745. The exterior of the castle reflects a Victorian make-over in 1863. Inside are wonderful artefacts, plasterwork and paintings.

THE TROSSACHS

An area of outstanding natural beauty in central Scotland, it has protected status as the main sector of the Loch Lomond and the Trossachs National Park. Scotland's first such designated park, its land stretches for 720 square miles (1,865 sq km) from the Argyll Forest Park in the west over to Callander in the east, and from Killin and Tyndrum in the north to Balloch in the south, at the foot of Loch Lomond. The Trossachs is the region lying to the east of Loch Lomond which was first 'discovered' by travellers in the late 18th century, and was popularised for a wider audience as a thrilling backdrop to the novels of Sir Walter Scott (1771–1832). Scott's famous poem, *The Lady of the Lake* (1810), was set in identifiable and accessible places across the Trossachs, and brought tourists to the area.

The village of Aberfoyle is the key to this region, giving easy access to the wooded hills of the Queen Elizabeth Forest Park and the peak of Ben Venue (729m/2,319ft), and Loch Katrine to the north. There are great opportunities for walking and cycling, including a pretty cycle route that runs through the Forest Park and continues along the shores of Loch Venachar and Loch Lubnaig to Balquhidder, Lochearnhead and Killin. The Trossachs Discovery visitor centre in Aberfoyle is a mine of information about activities in the area. The Scottish Wool Centre behind it offers a Sheepdog School Show, as well as a chance to see lambs and sheep shearing.

Loch Katrine, at the heart of the Trossachs, is a loch of clear water studded by islands and surrounded by woodland and mountains, and looks almost too good to be true. In fact, it serves central Glasgow with water, and part of its peaceful aspect comes from the fact that only one motorised boat is permitted upon its waters: the elegant old steamship, SS *Sir Walter Scott*. You can hire a bicycle at the pier and follow the northern shore of the loch.

PLACES OF INTEREST

Angus Folk Museum (NTS)
Kirkwynd, Glamis.
Tel: 01307 840288

Aviation Museum
Kirriemuir.
Tel: 01573 573233;
www.kamrafa.co.uk

J M Barrie's Birthplace (NTS)
9 Brechin Road, Kirriemuir.
Tel: 01575 572646

Bell's Blair Atholl Distillery
Pitlochry (at southern end of town).
Tel: 01796 482003

Bells Cherrybank Gardens
Perth. Tel: 01738 472800;
www.thecalyx.co.uk

Ben Lawers National Nature Reserve
Mountain Visitor Centre (NTS), off A827,
6 miles (9.7km) northeast of Killin.
Tel: 01567 820397

The Black Watch Regimental Museum
Balhousie Castle, North Inch, Perth.
Tel: 0131 310 8530

Blair Castle
Blair Atholl, just off A9.
Tel: 01796 481207;
www.blair-castle.co.uk

Branklyn Garden (NTS)
116 Dundee Road, Perth.
Tel: 01738 625535

Castle Menzies
Weem, by Aberfeldy.
Tel: 01887 820982

Dewar's World of Whisky
Aberfeldy Distillery, Aberfeldy.
Tel: 01887 822010;
www.dewarswow.com

RRS *Discovery*
Dundee. Tel: 01382 201245
www.rrsdiscovery.com

Doune Castle (HS)
Tel: 01786 841742

Drummond Castle Gardens
Muthill, Crieff.
Tel: 01764 681433;
www.drummoncastlegardens.co.uk

Earthquake House
Comrie.

Edradour Distillery
Pitlochry. Tel: 01796 472095;
www.edradour.co.uk

Famous Grouse Experience
The Hosh, Crieff.
Tel: 01764 656565;
www.famousgrouse.com

Frigate *Unicorn*
Discovery Point, Dundee.
Tel: 01382 200900;
www.frigateunicorn.org

Glamis Castle
Glamis. Tel: 01307 840393;
www.glamis-castle.co.uk

The Hermitage
by Dunkeld.
Tel: 01350 728641
Two miles (3km) west of Dunkeld.

Inchmahome Priory
Port of Menteith.
Tel: 01877 385294

Innerpeffray Library
5 miles from Crieff, off B8062.
Tel: 01764 652819;
www.innerpeffraylibrary.co.uk

Killiecrankie Visitor Centre
3 miles (5km) north of Pitlochry.
Tel: 01796 473233

Loch of the Lowes Visitor Centre
Off A923 northeast of Dunkeld.
Tel: 01350 727337;
www.swt.org.uk

Meigle Sculptured Stone Museum
Blairgowrie.
Tel: 01828 640612

Moirlanich Longhouse
Near to Killin. Tel: 01567 820988

Perth Museum & Art Gallery
78 George Street, Perth.
Tel: 01738 632488; www.perthshire.com

Queen's View Visitor Centre
7 miles (11.3km) west of Pitlochry on
B8019. Tel: 01796 473123;
www.forestry.gov.uk

Scone Palace
Scone, by Perth.
Tel: 01738 552300;
www.scone-palace.co.uk

Scottish Crannog Centre
South Loch Tay, Kenmore.
Tel: 01887 830583;
www.crannog.co.uk

Scottish Hydroelectric Visitor Centre
Pitlochry. Tel: 01796 473152;
www.aboutbritain.com/
HydroElectricVisitorCentre.htm

Scottish Wool Centre
Aberfoyle. Tel: 01877 382850

Verdant Works
West Henderson's Wynd, Dundee.
Tel: 01382 225282;
www.verdantworks.com

FOR CHILDREN

Beatrix Potter Exhibition & Garden
Birnham Institute, Station Road,
Birnham, by Dunkeld.
Tel: 01350 727674;
www.birnhaminstitute.com

Camperdown Wildlife Centre
Camperdown Country Park, Dundee.
Tel: 01382 431811;
www.dundeecity.gov.uk/camperdown

Drummond Trout Farm & Fishery
Comrie, off A85.
Tel: 01764 670500;
www.drummondtroutfarm.co.uk

Sensation: Dundee
Greenmarket, Dundee.
Tel: 01382 228800;
www.sensation.org.uk

PERFORMING ARTS

Dundee Contemporary Arts
152 Nethergate.
Tel: 01382 909900;
www.dca.org.uk

SHOPPING

Perth Farmers' Market
First Sat each month.

SPORTS & ACTIVITIES

ADVENTURE SPORTS

Croft-na-Caber
Kenmore, Loch Tay.
Tel: 01887 830588;
www.croftnacaber.com

Highland Adventure Safari
Drumdewan, Aberfeldy.
Tel: 01887 820071;
www.highlandadventuresafaris. co.uk

Loch Tay Boating Centre
Tel: 01887 830291;
www.loch-tay.co.uk

BOAT TRIPS

SS *Sir Walter Scott*
Trossachs Pier Complex.
Tel: 01877 376316;
www.lochkatrine.co.org

COUNTRY PARKS

Glengoulandie Country Park
8 miles (13km) northeast of Aberfeldy.
Tel: 01887 830495;
www.glengoulandie.co.uk

CYCLING

Escape Route
3 Atholl Road, Pitlochry.
Tel: 01796 473859;
www.escape-route.biz

Katrinewheelz
Trossachs Pier Complex, Loch Katrine.
Tel: 01877 376316;
www.lochkatrine.co.uk
FISHING
Lake of Menteith Fisheries
'Ryeyards', Port of Menteith.
Tel: 01877 385664;
www.menteith-fisheries.co.uk
GOLF
Crieff Golf Course
Ferntower, Perth Road.
Tel: 01764 652909; www.crieffgolf.co.uk
Gleneagles
Auchterarder. Tel: 01764 662231;
www.gleneagles.com
Pitlochry Golf Course
Golf Course Road, Pitlochry.
Tel: 01796 472792
HORSE-RIDING
Millhorn Farm Riding Centre
Roseount, Blairgowrie.
Tel: 01828 626172
WALKING
Cateran Trail
Circular trail from Blairgowrie,
64 miles (103km).
www.pkct.org/caterantrail

Loch Lomond and the Trossachs
National Park
www.lochlomond-trossachs.org
Rob Roy Way
Drymen to Pitlochry.
92 miles (148km).
www.robroyway.com

ANNUAL CUSTOMS & EVENTS
Blair Castle
Glenfiddich Piping Championships,
end Oct.
Atholl Gathering and Highland Games,
end May.
Comrie
Flambeaux Procession, 31 Dec.
Crieff
Highland Gathering, Aug.
Kirriemuir
Angus Glens Walking Festival,
early Jun.
Perth
Festival of the Arts, May.
Highland Games, Aug.
Pitlochry
Highland Games, Sep.

93

The Gleneagles Hotel

Auchterarder, PH3 1NF
Tel: 01764 662231
www.gleneagles.com

With an international reputation for high standards and its championship golf course, this grand hotel, close to the A9, is one of the finest in Scotland. It's main restaurant has a coveted four AA rosettes, but if dining here seems a little over the top (or beyond your budget), why not treat yourself to afternoon tea. If the standard package with delicious cakes, sandwiches, pastries and scones isn't enough, try the champagne version or even sample a whisky-taster's tea! Reservations are essential for weekends.

Perthshire Visitor Centre

Bankfoot, Perth, PH1 4EB
Tel: 01738 787696
www.macbeth.co.uk

Lying some 7 miles (11.3km) north of Perth on the A9, this busy centre is based around quality shopping. Stock up on Loch Fyne fresh salmon and oysters, Macsween's tasty, renowned haggis and locally made fruit wines before relaxing in the 120-seater restaurant, which serves a tempting combination of home baking and locally sourced produce.

The Watermill

Mill Street, Aberfeldy, PH15 2BG
Tel: 01887 822896
www.aberfeldywatermill.com

This extensive complex now includes a bookshop, music shop and art gallery all in a converted watermill, infused with the aroma of freshly brewed coffee. Enjoy a fruit smoothie on the terrace, or a speciality coffee with your cake – all the products are locally sourced or organic where possible. And the old waterwheel is still used to power the lighting!

ABERFELDY

PASS OF KILLICRANKIE

Almondbank Inn

31 Main Street, Almondbank, PH1 3NJ
Tel: 01738 583242

The views from the garden of this family-run pub, just 3 miles (4.8km) west of Perth, are wonderful, including the River Almond, famous for its trout and coarse fishing. Tuck into snacks or a high tea, or sample the dinner menu with its steaks, chicken, Mexican dishes and specials such as duck with wild berries. Children are welcome, and there's water for dogs.

Killiecrankie House Hotel

Killiecrankie, PH16 5LG
Tel: 01796 473220
www.killiecrankiehotel.co.uk

This sprawling country house hotel at the northern end of the Killiecrankie Pass offers great informal dining in its cosy, mahogany-panelled bar and conservatory. Try the home-cooked honey-roast ham salad, or perhaps a substantial game casserole.
The produce is local, and fruit and vegetables are fresh from the hotel's garden. Children and dogs welcome.

Moulin Hotel

11–13 Kirkmichael Road, Moulin,
PH16 5EW
Tel: 01796 472196
www.moulinhotel.co.uk

Just outside Pitlochry on the A924 stands this imposing old village inn, offering Highland hospitality, home-brewed beer and good food. It's at the foot of Ben Vrackie, so good walking country is on the doorstep. Food is served all day, with log fires lit in the winter and a lovely courtyard garden for summer. The menu might include sautéed mushroom pancakes and locally smoked lamb. In the pub's micro-brewery you can try local favourites such as Old Remedial.

OBAN BAY

Argyll, Mull & Western Highlands

ARDNAMURCHAN

MORVERN

ARRAN

CRINAN CANAL

DUNOON

GLASGOW

GLEN COE & RANNOCH MOOR

INVERARY

KILMARTIN

KINTYRE

LOCH LOMOND

LOCHGILPHEAD

MULL & IONA

OBAN

INTRODUCTION

The indentations of western Scotland's rugged coastline characterise this diverse region, with the grandeur and majesty of Glen Coe and the craggy mountains and valleys of the north contrasting with the more open, hilly landscapes of the south. Great sea lochs spread their narrowing fingers inland, creating isolated and island-bound communities, and havens for wildlife. There is ancient history to discover at Kilmartin and Iona, and industrial history in Scotland's vibrant second city, Glasgow.

HOT SPOTS

Unmissable attractions

Cruise across the still waters of Loch Lomond and visit popular Balloch Castle at its southern end...witness the scene of the bloody massacre of the Macdonald clan at Glen Coe...admire the rhododendron blooms in the gardens of Brodick Castle at the foot of Goatfell Mountain...attend the Cowal Highland Gathering at Dunoon where pipers come from all parts of the world to compete against each other...spend some time in cultural and cosmopolitan Glasgow and visit the ultra-modern Science Centre and the Glasgow Tower...look down from the viewing gallery upon the glass-making process at Caithness Glass...take a ferry to Iona from Tobermory harbour, on the Isle of Mull, to visit the ancient burial ground of King Macbeth.

1

2 Glen Coe
A lone piper plays a lament near the mountains of Glen Coe. It was at this spot in 1692 that 38 members of the Macdonald clan were murdered by their guests, on the orders of the government. The area has long been popular with walkers and climbers and now attracts skiers, too.

1 Loch Lomond
A panoramic view to the sparkling waters of Loch Lomond across the plain below Duncryne Hill, also known to locals as 'The Dumpling'.

3 Isle of Mull
The shore of Loch Na Keal on Mull. The open-sea loch is popular for birding. Minke whales, dolphins and porpoises visit in the summer.

4

4 Crinan Canal

The village of Cairnbaan sits at the edge of the Crinan Canal. Above the village are a series of, probably Iron Age, cup and ring marks in the rock, believed to have been carved about 4000 years ago.

5 Kilchurn Castle, Loch Awe

One of the most romantically situated castles in Scotland, the ruins of Kilchurn stand out on a peninsula on Loch Awe. What's left of the 15th-century castle can be reached by ferry or on foot.

6 Luma Light Factory, Glasgow

The distinctive 1930s art deco former light bulb factory has been converted into flats, but it retains the stylish glass tower as a staircase. Now known as the Luma Tower, the conversion has won several architectural awards.

5 6

ARDNAMURCHAN

ARDNAMURCHAN & MORVERN

You can go no further west on mainland Britain than Ardnamurchan Point, with its spectacular views over to Mull, Coll and Tiree. The whole peninsula, with its rocky hills and desolate moorland, gale-blown trees and pretty heather-capped promontories, has an 'end-of-the-world' feeling. The main road mostly hugs the northern shore of Loch Sunart, rich in birdlife, and you can take a minor road to Ardnamurchan's north coast as the main road passes round Beinn nan Losgann, or continue to the little crofting village of Kilchoan, where a ferry goes to Tobermory on Mull. The 13th-century Mingary Castle, built on its sheer cliff to guard the entrance to Loch Sunart, is the place where King James IV finally accepted the submission of the Lord of the Isles in 1495; Hanoverian troops built barracks inside it 350 years later.

It's worthwhile making a detour to Sanna Bay for magnificent views to Muck, Rum and Canna and for superb wild flowers by the beach. A lighthouse stands guard on the furthest tip of the peninsula, with access inside in summer – it's a good place for spotting seals and otters, if you're lucky.

Morvern, across Loch Sunart, is a rugged land with gentler green glens. Lochaline, a popular yachting haven, is reached either by road along Glen Gleann, or by ferry from the Isle of Mull. There are two castles to visit in the area – the remains of Ardtornish, east of the village, and well-preserved Kinlochaline at the head of Loch Aline. The silica sands at Lochaline have been quarried commercially for manufacturing optical glass. Fiunary, along the Sound of Mull, was the birthplace of George Macleod, founder of the Iona Community. Caisteal nan Con is a small fortress guarding the Sound of Mull. The road ends some 4 miles (6.4km) beyond, near Drimnin, with views towards Tobermory.

Insight

BRUCE AND THE SPIDER

In 1307, on his way back from exile on Rathlin Island, off Northern Ireland, Robert the Bruce mustered his troops in Glen Cloy, on Arran, before heading to the Scottish mainland to try once more to oust the English and claim the throne. According to legend, he was roused from despair and inspired to fight once more – and succeed this time – by watching a spider, spinning its web and succeeding only on the seventh attempt to attach its thread. In another version of the story, he watched the spider in a cave near to Blackwaterfoot on Arran, known to this day as the King's Caves.

ARRAN, ISLE OF

Generations of Clydesiders have enjoyed holidays on this scenically attractive island, caught between the Ayrshire coast and the Kintyre Peninsula, yet it remains largely unspoiled. The Highland Boundary Fault runs through the island, and while the mountain of Goat Fell (874m/2,867ft) dominates the skyline to the north, the south is much more level. This reflects the geology of the country as a whole, and Arran is often tagged 'Scotland in Miniature'. Glen Rosa offers fairly easy walking, while Goat Fell and Glen Sannox are more rugged, and there are plenty of opportunities for a range of other outdoor activities, including golf and pony trekking, around the island. Brodick is the biggest town, with villages catering for visitors scattered round the superb 56-mile (90km) coastline.

The red sandstone Brodick Castle is the island's biggest single attraction, with its extensive collection of porcelain and silver, some 19th-century sporting pictures and trophies, and beautiful country park of meadows and woodland. The gardens include a world-renowned collection of rhododendrons. The seat of the Dukes of Hamilton, the estate has a history that dates back 800 years.

The legacy of much earlier settlers may be seen in the chambered cairns at Clachaig, Whiting Bay and other sites, and also in the stone circles on Machrie Moor. The standing stones date from the Bronze Age but there is also evidence that the site was previously occupied in the Neolithic era.

In recent years the island has developed a name for its food produce, which includes cheese and smoked meats. Around the courtyard of Home Farm, just north of Brodick, you can see the cheese being made at the superb Island Cheese Company, and you can purchase delicately smoked fish, rich game and free-range poultry next door at Creelers Smokehouse (or sample it in Creeler's Seafood Restaurant). The fragrant soaps of Arran Aromatics share the same site. Arran Fine Foods, at Lamlash, sells a range of locally produced mustards and preserves. The island's distillery, based at Lochranza only opened in the 1990s.

Ferries to Arran operate from Ardrossan (year-round) and Claonaig, by Skipness (summer). The Ayrshire coast between here and Prestwick Airport is famous worldwide for the quality of its golf courses, centring on Troon.

Visit

LANGUAGE OF THE LAND

In Scotland lakes are lochs, and 'ben' means mountain. Like many Highland place names, these are ancient Gaelic words, and often give you a pretty good idea of the kind of place they refer to – 'kin' (Gaelic ceann), for example, means head, so Kinloch means the top of a lake, while 'inver' (inbhir) denotes an outlet – Inverness is where the River Ness meets the sea. 'Tarbert' (or 'Tarbet') means isthmus or crossing place. Other pointers include 'ard', a height, 'ban' meaning white; 'beg', confusingly meaning little, and 'more', meaning great. It all adds another dimension to this rich and culturally diverse landscape.

CRINAN CANAL

In 1847 Queen Victoria and Prince Albert sailed the 9 miles (14.5km) of the Crinan Canal aboard the barge *Sunbeam* – a journey followed later in the century by MacBrayne's steamers in order to sell 'Royal Route' excursions from Glasgow to Oban. Today you are most likely to see pleasure craft negotiating the canal's 15 locks, but its original purpose was to enable merchant traffic to and from the Western Isles to avoid the hazardous voyage around the Mull of Kintyre. Two famous engineers worked on the Crinan Canal, which opened in 1801. John Rennie was responsible for the original engineering work, and Thomas Telford solved problems with the water supply.

From the basin at Ardrishaig, where it leaves Loch Fyne, the canal hugs the wooded hillsides as it climbs up to its highest point of 64 feet (19.4m). On the hills above Cairnbaan are reservoirs that constantly replenish the water down in the canal as it descends underneath the unusual hand-wound rolling bridge at Dunadry. Beyond this the landscape then opens out into the flat marshland near to the River Add estuary. The canal ends at the picturesque Crinan Harbour, with views over the Sound of Jura. With some luck you may find a 'puffer' in the harbour to remind you of the canal's past glories.

DUNOON

Paddle steamers used to bring huge crowds from Gourock to Dunoon, and there are still regular ferry services here. On the grassy headland between the town's two bays are the remains of the 13th-century castle, largely destroyed in 1685. Below is the 1896 statue of Burns's love, Highland Mary, erected to mark the centenary of the poet's death. Dunoon is busiest each year during late August for the prestigious Cowal Highland Gathering, when more than 150 pipe bands from all over the world.

DUNOON

DUNOON

Morag's Fairy Glen, off the road south from Dunoon, has shaded walks along the Berry Burn, but for more expansive views, continue onward to Toward Point lighthouse (not open) at the southern end of the A815, where you can look out across the water to Bute and down to Largs. In the grounds of the stout 19th-century Castle Toward, now an education centre, is a ruined 15th-century tower house, somewhat confusingly called Toward Castle.

One of the most vile atrocities of the Civil War began here, when Campbell of Ardkinglas besieged the Lamonts, who were Stuart loyalists. Although guaranteed safety, 36 Lamont men were taken to Dunoon and hanged – a monument in Tom-a-Mhoid Road marks the place.

Just north of Dunoon at Lochan Wood is the attractive Cowal Bird Garden, and this area is rich in ancient sites. Near Sandbank, on the shore of Holy Loch, are the huge stones forming Adam's Grave, a remaining Neolithic burial chamber,

and you can take a trail from near Ardnadam Farm to see the ancient field boundaries and the site of a prehistoric enclosure.

Bute has been the holiday playground for generations of Glaswegians, most of whom arrive at Rothesay on the ferry from Wemyss Bay. Stood on the Firth of Clyde, Rothesay has a late 19th-century atmosphere created by its solid, mostly Victorian houses and decorative Winter Gardens, but much more ancient are the impressive ruins of the moated and circular 13th-century Rothesay Castle, where some restoration took place in the 19th and 20th centuries.

The island largely consists of green and fertile hills, with superb views across the narrow Kyles of Bute to the mainland and to mountainous Arran. Just off the east coast road is one of Bute's hidden gems, the extraordinary Victorian Gothic Mount Stuart House, surrounded by extensive gardens that lead down to the shore.

GLASGOW

Scotland's second city, Glasgow grew on the back of the tobacco trade with the New World to become one of the major industrial and engineering centres of Britain in the 19th century. In the 20th century its fortunes changed, as ship-building and manufacturing slumped after World War II. In recent years, however, it has reinvented itself as a vibrant and stylish place to be, making the most of its Victorian heritage of buildings, celebrating the designs of its most famous son, Charles Rennie Mackintosh (1868–1928), and investing in daring new projects that include the 'Armadillo' Scottish Exhibition and Conference Centre and the titanium-clad Science Centre. The trendy bars, cafés and restaurants spill out onto the pavements, and the city is known across the world for its classy shopping malls selling everything from top quality furniture to luxury chocolate, designer fashion, in addition to hand-crafted jewellery.

Glasgow is full of things to do and see. Highlights include the treasures on show in the newly reopened Kelvingrove Museum; the fabulous Science Centre, with around 500 interactive exhibits to explain everything from the structure of the Forth Bridge to the movement of an artificial limb; and the People's Palace – the red-brick museum of local life on Glasgow Green which captures the wit, eccentricity and gritty character of the city, telling its history through familiar objects and quotes from real people. South of the city centre, in leafy Pollok Park, is Glasgow's outstanding art collection, made by shipping magnate William Burrell, and displaying a small range of exquisite pieces – from original paintings to Chinese porcelain to some medieval tapestries and stained glass – in a small, purpose-built gallery. Musts on the Mackintosh trail include Glasgow School of Art, the House for an Art Lover, the Mackintosh House at the university's Hunterian

GLASGOW

GLEN COE

Museum, and the famous Willow Tea Rooms. The Kibble Palace, a vast Victorian glasshouse in the Botanic Gardens of the West End, is the perfect escape on a wet or chilly day.

GLEN COE & RANNOCH MOOR

On 13 February 1692 the Campbells clan defied the age-old traditions of Highland hospitality and massacred 38 members of the Macdonald clan in Glen Coe. Alastair Macdonald, like many clansmen reluctant to accept William and Mary as ruling monarchs, failed to get papers attesting his loyalty to a magistrate by the deadline, the end of 1691, though they did arrive in Edinburgh in the new year. However, the papers were secretly suppressed by the Under Secretary of State, who then told Campbell of Glenlyon that the Macdonalds 'must all be slaughtered'. Campbell and his men, pretending to be delayed on a journey, were accommodated by the Macdonalds in Glen Coe then cold-bloodedly slaughtered their hosts.

Activity

GOING DOWNHILL FAST

Glen Coe's skiing may not be as fashionable as Klosters' in Switzerland, but it can be just as exciting. From White Corries at the top of the glen, where the fascinating Museum of Scottish Skiing and Mountaineering puts the sport into perspective, a chairlift takes skiers (and summer visitors) high into the mountains, where there are superb views to Rannoch Moor and beyond. There are 15 runs catering for all abilities, some with intriguing names – Fly Paper, for example, and Mug's Alley. Instruction is available. If hurtling downhill doesn't appeal, the Glen Coe area offers cross-country skiing, ski mountaineering, snowboarding, speed skating, and even paragliding.

The atrocity took place in the lower glen by Glencoe village, where the now heather-roofed Folk Museum offers displays of real Highland life. The most dramatic part of Glen Coe is higher up. From

121

GLEN COE

the roof of the National Trust for Scotland Visitor Centre there is a fine view of outstanding mountain scenery of stark peaks and glittering waterfalls. You can get details about the many exhilarating walks from the Visitor Centre; there is challenging climbing, too, for experienced climbers.

Southeast of Glen Coe, Rannoch Moor is a vast expanse of peat bog, treacherous even in the driest season. Rannoch actually means 'watery' in Gaelic. The finest view is perhaps from the railway as it crosses on its way north to Fort William, but the best approach by car is along Loch Rannoch. On its south side is the Black Wood of Rannoch, native Caledonian forest of ancient pines and groves of alder, birch and juniper. Just beyond Bridge of Gaur is a house built as barracks for Hanoverian troops after Culloden – a bleak posting. Rannoch Station is the end of the road, though it is possible to walk from here on old tracks. In places you will come across the blackened stumps of ancient trees protruding from the peat – evidence that this forlorn place was once covered in forest.

INVERARAY

Inveraray is the seat of the Duke of Aygyll, chieftain of the Clan Campbell. Set on the shores of Loch Fyne, Inveraray is as fine an example of town planning as you will find, created by the 3rd Duke of Argyll in the 1740s to sit at the gates of his grand new home. It seems a great deal of trouble to go to, just to move your ancestral home by 0.5 mile (0.8km), but this was, after all, the extravagant 18th century. The little town that the Duke created is stylish, with a wide main street of white-painted houses running up to the classical kirk. Down at the waterfront are brilliant white arches, one of which leads up to All Saints Episcopal Church – climb the bell-tower for a wonderful panoramic view of the town, the castle, the loch and the hills.

Inveraray Castle, now home to the current 12th Duke and his family, is a neo-Gothic building with pointed sash windows and battlements. Inside, its most spectacular feature is the Armoury Hall, the tallest room in Scotland, which is dramatically adorned with pikes, axes, swords and muskets. A walking tour of the castle includes splendid state rooms with ornate gilded plasterwork, fine furniture and some fine Campbell family portraits.

Moored on the loch side is the three-masted vessel Arctic Penguin, upon which you can take a turn at steering, ring the ship's telegraph, visit the engine room and watch archive film of old sailing and steam ships. Inveraray Jail, near the kirk, has opened its doors to willing visitors. In the semi-circular courtroom you can be part of the crowd hearing a trial, and in the 19th-century cells you can try out canvas hammocks and turn the crank machine. You can even see mug-shots of petty criminals.

KILMARTIN

The waters of Loch Awe once flowed southwards through the glacier-formed Kilmartin Glen, depositing sediment on the valley floor. The area was occupied by farmers from early prehistoric times, and the concentration of monuments that they left behind makes this one of the richest archaeological areas in Scotland. At Achnabreck is the largest group of cup-and-ring marked rocks in Britain, but even more impressive remains are to be found further north.

The tall, flat-faced Ballymeanoch standing stones and a line of burial cairns stretch towards Kilmartin village. Ri Cruin is a crescent of boulders in a grove, and carvings of axeheads and, possibly, a boat's keel can be seen on the stones. The three Nether Largie cairns are higher – especially the most southerly, with its large chamber topped by huge stone slabs. Central to the site is Temple Wood Circle, begun around 3000 BC and modified several times

LOCH LOMOND

Visit

DALRIADA

From around AD 500 the Scottish kingdom of Dalriada had its capital in the hill fort at Dunadd. There are traces of ancient buildings on the hillside and defensive terraces that can be seen around the summit. Carved in the rock a little way outside is an inscription in Ogham script, which is evidence of Pictish use of the hilltop as well as a basin and a footprint that may have been used at coronations. Some people believe that Aidan was crowned first Christian king in Britain here in AD 574 by St Columba, and that the stone used became the Stone of Scone, once in Westminster Abbey but now safe and on display in Edinburgh Castle.

up to 1200 BC. To get the most out of this fascinating area head over to the superb interpretative museum in Kilmartin village, where there is also an extensive collection of carved 9th- to 16th-century grave slabs in the churchyard.

Carnasserie Castle, further up the valley, is a well-preserved fortified house from the 16th century.

KINTYRE

At the north end of Kintyre and 38 miles (61km) from Campbeltown, the pretty fishing port of Tarbert has rows of colour-washed houses and the remains of a 15th-century tower house built on the site of a former royal castle. The Campbeltown road follows the wind-swept west fringe of Kintyre, with wide views over to Jura and Islay, and then the hills give way to a gentler landscape towards the handsome harbour of Campbeltown. By the waterfront is the 15th-century Campbeltown Cross, and near by is an unexpected delight – the 1913 art deco front of the 256-seat Picture House. Davaar Island, reached on foot at low tide, shelters the harbour, and on its south side is a magnificent restored cave-painting of the crucifixion, originally created by Archibald MacKinnon in 1887.

St Columba landed near Southend at the foot of the peninsula – a ruined chapel and two footprints carved in a nearby rock mark the spot. A winding road eastwards goes to the Mull of Kintyre, with its lighthouse – a stark, windswept place, only 12 miles (19.5km) from Ireland. A single-track, hairpin road with breathtaking views over Arran follows the western coast back to Campbeltown; alternatively retrace your route up the B842, diverting west to the superb sands of Machrihanish, where the golf course is on the bay's edge.

To the north of Campbeltown, the east coast route is slow and winding, with tree-lined glens and fertile valleys. Up the valley from the battlemented castle by the shore at Saddell (now let by the Landmark Trust) are the remains of Saddell Abbey, with its impressive collection of carved gravestones (open access). Carradale, further up the coast, is a small rural village beside a beautiful sandy bay. You can catch the summer ferry from Claonaig to Lochranza on Arran, and at Skipness you can explore the fine castle ruins or wander around the 13th-century Kilbrannan Chapel.

LOCHGILPHEAD

Lochgilphead was once the centre of herring fishing on Loch Gilp, with a wooden pier stretched across the bay, but the fish mysteriously vanished before World War I. Mills and dyeworks also disappeared, and, besides tourism centred around the Crinan Canal, the main employer is now Argyll and Bute Council, which has rather grand headquarters at Kilmory Castle.

The castle gardens, now open to the public, were partly laid out by Joseph Hooker, first director of Kew Gardens. They are full of rare rhododendrons, as is Crarae Garden, on the Inveraray road, which is planted round a spectacular gorge. A little further to the north is Auchindrain Township, a former

crofting settlement which now gives visitors an experience of Highland life. Its houses have original furniture and the barns are equipped with old implements.

Glacial action reversed the waters of Loch Awe, to the north of Lochgilphead, to flow through the dramatic Pass of Brander instead of through Kilmartin Glen. The longest loch in Scotland – measuring nearly 25 miles (40km), more than a mile (1.6km) longer than Loch Ness – it is very narrow, and the north end is dominated by the peak of Ben Cruachan. You can take a steamboat trip from Lochawe village which includes the impressive ruins of Kilchurn Castle. Ardanaiseig Gardens, surrounding a beautiful old hotel and beside the western shore of the loch, are full of glowing rhododendrons and specimen trees. It is worth following the minor road south through Inverliever Forest, which offers many forest walks and some spectacular high viewpoints over the loch. The eastern shore

road gives views of the loch's small islands, some with ancient chapels and burial grounds.

LOCH LOMOND

Part of Scotland's first National Park (Loch Lomond and the Trossachs National Park was established in 2002), Loch Lomond has two very distinct characters – the narrow upper loch is hemmed in by grand mountains, and stretches up into the heart of the Highlands, while the broad, island-speckled southern end is bordered by fertile farmland. Here, within easy reach of Glasgow, are some of the loch's most popular tourist attractions.

Balloch, with its modern castle, country park and opportunities for boat cruises, sits astride the only natural outlet from the loch, and is a popular centre. The Loch Lomond Shores Visitor Centre includes an information centre and shopping outlets. Up the west side, off the well-used A82, is Luss, a smart estate village.

135

Insight

MOUNTAIN POWER

Ben Cruachan holds a secret – Scotland's first big pump storage power station. The Visitor Centre explains how water from an artificial loch high up on the mountain is fed down through the rock to turbines within the mountain. Off-peak power is used to pump the water back up to the reservoir. The highlight of any visit is a 0.75-mile (1.2km) ride down tunnels to the huge turbine hall, 300 feet (91.5m) long and 120 feet (36.5m) high. The plants along the way are real – tropical species, which are thriving happily in the artificial light, heat and humidity of the tunnels.

Lomond's east side is much quieter, offering walking and outdoor pursuits. From Balmaha there are some good views over several of the loch's 38 named islands – especially Inchcailloch, once the site of a nunnery, and now part of the Loch Lomond National Nature Reserve. Much of the eastern shore is within the 50,000-acre (20,000ha) Queen Elizabeth Forest Park. The narrow road ends at Rowardennan, from where there is a stiff climb up the 3,192 feet (973m) of Ben Lomond. To visit the beautiful Inversnaid, approach from Aberfoyle or by ferry from Inveruglas – unless you are energetic enough for the walk along the West Highland Way from Rowardennan.

It is on the shores of Loch Lomond that the 95-mile (153km) West Highland Way, Scotland's first long-distance footpath, makes the transition from easy lowland walking to the more rugged terrain of the Highlands. Starting from Milngavie (pronounced Mull-guy) on the outskirts of Glasgow, the route makes its way north to Fort William, often using ancient and historic routes – drove roads by which cattle dealers reached market (like the Devil's Staircase out of Glen Coe), military roads instituted by General Wade to aid in suppressing the clans, old coaching roads and even discarded railway lines. Walk all the way if you wish – experts recommend going south to north, to build up stamina for the hills – or take a short walk along the route; there is no shortage of breath-taking sections, and you may see red deer and, just possibly, golden eagles on the way.

MULL & IONA

Take the time to explore and discover Mull and you will find it full of interest and beauty. Craignure is the main arrival point, and from Old Pier Station the Mull and West Highland Narrow Gauge Railway runs the extremely scenic 1.25 miles (2km) to Torosay Castle. This line boasts a real rarity – a modern steam locomotive, built in Sheffield in 1993.

Torosay Castle is actually a Victorian mansion, set in 12 acres (5ha) of superb gardens. The house is full of character and is enthusiastically shared with all visitors by its resident owner – you are positively encouraged to sit

on chairs, peer into cupboards and browse through the family scrapbooks. Near by, on a craggy point with wonderful views along the Sound of Mull, is 13th-century Duart Castle, centre for the Clan Maclean.

Mountains give way to pretty pastoral scenery on the way to the little island's capital, Tobermory, with its houses painted in jolly colours around the bay – a familiar sight to fans of TV's *Balamory* for young children. Tobermory's tourist attractions – the Mull Museum and the distillery – are tiny. Calgary, further on, has an interesting sculpture trail and the best sandy beach on the island.

West of Ben More, Mull's highest mountain, is the Ardmeanach peninsula, the tip of which is only accessible by an arduous 5.5-mile (9km) path. Its main sight is MacCulloch's Tree, 50 feet (15m) high and engulfed in lava more than 50 million years ago. Boat trips round Mull sometimes give passengers a view of it.

137

Mull's main road is mostly single track and traverses the moorland from the east coast to Loch Scridain, and on across the Ross of Mull to Fionnphort, for the Iona ferry. South of the road is fine walking country, with a coastline of basalt stacks and sea arches – wild and lonely, and full of fascinating wildlife.

Iona is a magical place. Most visitors make straight for the abbey, but you should spare time for the remains of the 13th-century priory, built for the use of Augustinian nuns. St Columba founded his monastery in AD 563 where the abbey now stands, and from it the teachings of Christianity radiated throughout Europe. The monks compiled a library of illuminated manuscripts including the *Book of Kells*, now on show in Dublin's Trinity College Library. At the centre of Columba's settlement was a church of oak logs and thatch, and, around it, huts for the individual monks. Columba himself slept on the bedrock with a stone for a pillow. Larger huts of wattle were used as a dining hall, guest house, library and writing room. The monks' lives consisted of prayer, simple farming and study, and here Columba poetry in Latin and Irish.

Columba's foundation ended in AD 806 when Vikings slew 68 monks at Martyrs' Bay. Later a church and buildings erected there by 12th-century Benedictine monks were left in ruins after the Reformation, until restoration began in 1910. Currently the home of the Iona Community, founded in 1938, the abbey welcomes pilgrims. Right beside it is the ancient burial ground of the Scottish kings, among them notably Macbeth and Duncan. The abbey does get busy with visitors at times, but although the island is small, it is possible to escape the crowds quickly and enjoy fine sands and rocky landscape, wild flowers and birds, and far-reaching sea views.

Many visitors will know of Staffa because of composer Mendelssohn's *Fingal's Cave* overture. He came

MULL

OBAN

to the island in 1829, to visit the cavern on its south side. Here, the dark volcanic basalt has cooled and formed its characteristic six-sided columns, making it look like a massive cathedral organ. The enormous interior of Fingal's Cave is also like a cathedral; weather permitting, visitors can land from some of the boat trips in the area.

OBAN

To experience the true splendour of Oban, you should climb at dusk to MacCaig's improbable Gothic Coliseum and watch the glorious sunset over the Firth of Lorne and the mountains of Morvern and Mull. MacCaig engaged unemployed stonemasons on his spectacular tower from around 1897, and though it was never finished, it is Oban's most notable landmark. At its foot, the bay, sheltered by the island of Kerrera, is busy with pleasure craft.

Much of the broad harbour front is dominated by hotels, and ferries for the Hebrides depart from

SPANISH TREASURE

There is an intriguing old treasure map, now on display at Inveraray Castle, showing the location of the shipwreck of a Spanish galleon that sank in Tobermory Bay in 1588. After the defeat of the Armada, many Spaniards attempted to get home via the north of Scotland.

The legend goes that one such vessel was given supplies for their voyage by the inhabitants of Mull, but the Spanish refused to pay for the supplies, and even locked up Donald Maclean, who had come to collect the payment. He managed to escape, and, in retaliation, blew up the ship, which sank in the bay.

Confusion reigns as to whether the ship was a troop carrier, the *San Juan de Sicilia*, or a treasure ship, the *Florida*.

Another theory is that the English sent agents who destroyed the vessel. Treasure hunters are ever hopeful, and still dive here in search of a shower of golden ducats, yet so far only a few coins and a cannon have been raised from the murky depths of the bay.

Insight

FERRY CONVENIENT

You can't get too far in this part of Western Scotland without needing to catch a ferry over the water, especially to its 130 or so inhabited islands. Many of the shorter routes are operated by local owners and provide an excellent service, but Caledonian MacBrayne – CalMac – is undoubtedly the name you will come across most in this part of Scotland.

The company was formed in 1973 when MacBraynes, operators of shipping services mostly to the Western Isles since 1851, joined forces with the Clyde-based Caledonian Steam Packet Company, which was founded in 1889.

The CalMac ferry company sails to an impressive 22 islands and operates more than 29 ferries in a huge range of sizes, from the largest vessels working the Ullapool to Stornoway route, capable of taking 690 passengers and 123 cars, to the neat-sized six-car ferries that ply the scenic route from Oban to Lismore and from Ballycastle in Northern Ireland to Rathlin Island.

Railway Quay. Here, too, is Caithness Glass where you can see jewel-like paperweights being made, and buy them, of course. Oban Distillery, set in the heart of the town, welcomes visitors, and near by you'll find Geoffrey (Tailor) weaving tartans.

Northwards, the soaring tower of St Columba's Cathedral dominates the bay, and beyond it are the haunting remains of Dunollie Castle. A few miles further on, Dunstaffnage Castle, a mostly ruined stronghold with gatehouse, two round towers and 10-foot (3m) thick walls, stands on a rocky outcrop, and was once the prison of Flora Macdonald.

Across the Connel Bridge in the little town of Barcaldine is the Scottish Sea Life Sanctuary, where you can see British marine life at close quarters. South of the town is the Oban Rare Breeds Farm Park with farm animals, woodland walks and a pets' area. From here, drive on to Arduaine Garden with its superb collection of rhododendrons and wonderful views to the Isle of Jura.

OBAN

Caledonia

PLACES OF INTEREST

Ardanaiseig Gardens
Ardanaiseig Hotel, Kilchrenan.
Tel: 01866 833333;
www.ardanaiseig.com

Arduaine Garden
20 miles (32km) south of Oban,
on A816.
Tel: 01852 200366

Ardnamurchan Lighthouse Visitor Centre
Ardnamurchan Point, west of
Fort William.
Tel: 01972 510210

Auchindrain Township Open Air Museum
On A83, south of Inveraray.
Tel: 01499 500235;
www.auchindrainmuseum.org

Balloch Castle Country Park
Balloch. Tel: 01389 722600

Benmore Botanic Garden
7 miles (11km) north of Dunoon
on A815.
Tel: 01369 706261;
www.rbge.org.uk

Bonawe Iron Furnace
Taynuilt. Tel: 01866 822432

Botanic Gardens
Great Western Road, Glasgow.
Tel: 0141 334 2422

Brodick Castle, Garden & Country Park
Brodick, Isle of Arran.
Tel: 01770 302202

Burrell Collection
Pollok Country Park, Glasgow.
Tel: 0141 287 2550;
www.glasgowmuseums.com

Carnasserie Castle
2 miles (3km) north of Kilmartin,
off A816.

Crarae Garden
Visitor Centre and garden. Crarae.
Tel: 01546 886614

Cruachan Power Station Visitor Centre
Dalmally. Tel:01866 822618;
www.visitcruachan.co.uk

Duart Castle
South of Craignure, Isle of Mull,
off A849.
Tel: 01680 812319;
www.duartcastle.com

Dunadd Fort
Kilmartin Glen.

Dunstaffnage Castle
4 miles (6.5km) north of Oban,
off A85.
Tel: 01631 562465

Glasgow School of Art
167 Renfrew Street, Glasgow.
Tel: 0141 353 4526; www.gsa.ac.uk

Glencoe & North Lorn Folk Museum
Glencoe, Ballaculish.
Tel: 01855 811664

Glencoe Visitor Centre
Glencoe. Tel: 01855 811307

House for an Art Lover
Bellahouston Park,
10 Dumbreck Road, Glasgow.
Tel: 0141 353 4770;
www.houseforanartlover.co.uk

Inveraray Castle
Inverarary. Tel: 01499 302203;
www.inveraray-castle.com

Isle of Arran Distillery Visitor Centre
Lochranza, Arran.
Tel: 01770 830264;
www.arranwhisky.com

Kelvingrove Art Gallery & Museum
Argyle Street, Glasgow.
Tel: 0141 287 2699;
www.glasgowmuseums.com

Kilchurn Castle
Loch Awe. Tel: 01866 833333

Kilmartin House Museum
Kilmartin. Tel: 01546 510278;
www.kilmartin.org

Kilmory Castle Gardens
Lochgilphead. Tel: 01546 602127;
www.argyll-bute.gov.uk

Mount Stewart House
Rothesay, Bute.
Tel: 01700 503877;
www.mountstewart.com

Mull Museum
Main Street, Tobermory, Mull.

Oban Distillery
Stafford Street, Oban.
Tel: 01540 672219; www.malts.com

People's Palace
Glasgow Green, Glasgow.
Tel: 0141 554 0223;
www.glasgowmuseums.com

Rothesay Castle
Castlehill Street, Rothesay, Bute.
Tel: 01700 502691

Torosay Castle and Gardens
Mull. One mile (1.6km) south of
Craignure.
Tel: 01680 812421

145

FOR CHILDREN

Arctic Penguin (Inveraray Maritime Experience)
The Pier, Inveraray.
Tel: 01499 302213;
www.inveraraypier.com

Cowal Bird Garden
Lochan Wood, Sandbank Road,
Dunoon. Tel: 01369 707999

Glasgow Science Centre
50 Pacific Quay, Glasgow.
Tel: 0141 420 5000;
www.gsc.org.uk

Inveraray Jail
Church Square, Inveraray.
Tel: 01499 302381;
www.inverarayjail.co.uk

Oban Rare Breeds Farm Park
Glencruitten, by Oban.
Tel: 01631 770608;
www.obanrarebreeds.com

Scottish Sea Life Sanctuary
Off A828, on shore of Loch Creran,
Barcaldine.
Tel: 01631 720386;
www.sealsanctuary.co.uk

SHOPPING

Arran Fine Foods
The Old Mill, Lamlash, Arran.
Tel: 01770 600606;
www.paterson-arran.com

Creelers Smokehouse
Home Farm, Brodick, Arran.
Tel: 01770 302797;
www.creelers.co.uk

Dunoon Ceramics
Pot Shop, 162 Argyll Street, Dunoon.
Tel: 01369 704360

Geoffrey (Tailor) Kiltmakers & Weavers
309 Sauchiehall Street, Glasgow.
Tel: 0141 331 2388;
www.geoffreykilts.co.uk

Inverawe Smokehouses
Taynuilt.
Tel: 01866 822446;
www.smoked-salmon.co.uk

Island Cheese Company
Home Farm, Brodick, Arran.
Tel: 01770 302788;
www.islandcheese.co.uk

Loch Fyne Oyster Bar & Seafood Shop
Cairndow.
Tel: 01499 600264;
www.lochfyne.com
Loch Lomond Shores
Ben Lomond Way, Balloch.
Tel: 01389 721500;
www.lochlomondshores.com
Tiso Glasgow Outdoor Experience
50 Couper Street, Glasgow.
Tel: 0141 559 5450;
www.tiso.com

SPORTS & ACTIVITIES
ADVENTURE SPORTS
Puffin Dive Centre
Port Gallanach, south of Oban.
Tel: 01631 571190;
www.puffin.org.uk
Quadmania Ltd
Stronchullin Farm, Blairmore, Dunoon.
Tel: 01369 810289;
www.quadmaniascotland.co.uk
Lomond Adventure
Balmaha House, Balmaha.
Tel: 01360 870218

BOAT TRIPS
Cruise Loch Lomond Ltd
The Boat Yard, Tarbet, Loch Lomond.
Tel: 01301 702356;
www.cruiselochlomond.co.uk
Loch Etive Cruises
Etive View, Taynuilt.
Tel: 01866 822430
Macfarlane & Son
The Boatyard, Balmaha.
Tel: 01360 870214;
www.balmahaboatyard.co.uk
Waverley Excursions Ltd
33 Landsfield Quay, Glasgow.
Tel: 0845 1304647;
www.waverleyexcursions.co.uk
CYCLING
Crinan Cycles
Canal Basin Yard, Ardrishaig.
Tel: 01546 603511
Luing Bike Hire
Sunnybrae, South Cuan, Luing,
by Oban.
Tel: 01852 314274;
www.luingbikehire.co.uk
Explore the low-lying island by bike.

GOLF

Cowal Golf Club
Dunoon, off A815 at Kirn.
Tel: 01369 705673;
www.cowalgolfclub.com
18-hole course.

Craignure Golf Club
1 mile (1.6km) north of Craignure, Mull.
Tel: 01680 300420; www.golf.mag.
com/craignure. 9-hole course.

Kyles of Bute Golf Club
The Moss, Kames, Tighnabruaich.
Tel: 01700 811603
9-hole course.

Loch Lomond Golf Club
Rossdhu House, Luss.
Tel: 01436 655555;
www.lochlomond.com
18-hole course.

Machrihanish Golf Club
Machrihanish, north of Campbelltown.
Tel: 01586 810213; www.machgolf.com
18-hole course.

Tobermory Golf Club
Erray Road, Tobermory, Mull.
Tel: 01688 302338;
www.tobermoraygolfclub.com
9-hole course.

HORSE-RIDING

Apaloosa Holidays
Craobh Haven, by Lochgilphead.
Tel: 01852 500632

Argyll Riding
Dalchenna, Inveraray.
Tel: 01499 302611;
www.horserides.com

Argyll Trail Riding & Castle Riding Centre
Brenfield Farm, Ardrishaig.
Tel: 01546 603274; www.brenfield.co.uk

LONG-DISTANCE FOOTPATHS

Cowal Way
Partially way-marked trail
on Cowal Peninsula, 47 miles (75km).
www.colglen.co.uk

Isle of Arran Coastal Way
Circular route, 65 miles (104km).
www.coastalway.co.uk

Kintyre Way
New footpath developed to run from
Tarbet to Southend, 90 miles (60km).
www.kintyre.org

West Highland Way
Scotland's most famous long distance
trail, Glasgow to Fort William, 95 miles
(150km). www.west-highland-way.co.uk

WILDLIFE TOURS
Discover Mull
Ardrioch Farm, Dervaig, Mull.
Tel: 01688 400415;
www.discovermull.co.uk
Island Encounter
Arla Beag, Aros, Mull.
Tel: 01680 300441;
www.mullwildlife.co.uk
Wildlife tours of the island, including eagles, owls, otters and more. Advance booking essential.
Sea.fari
Easdale Harbour, Seil, by Oban.
Tel: 01852 300003; www.seafari.co.uk
Wildlife safaris in rigid inflatables.
Turus Mara
Penmore Hill, Dervaig, Mull.
Tel: 01688 400242;
www.turusmara.com.
Cruise tours from Ulva Ferry, Mull, or Oban, to Treshnish Isles, Staffa and Iona.

WINTER SPORTS
Glencoe Ski Centre
Kingshouse, Glencoe.
Tel: 0871 871 9929;
www.glencoemountain.com

The Ice Factor
Leven Road, Kinlochleven.
Tel: 01855 831100;
www.ice-factor.co.uk

ANNUAL EVENTS & CUSTOMS
Dunoon
Cowal Highland Gathering, late Aug.
Glasgow
Celtic Connections, folk music festival, Jan.
International Jazz Festival, early Jul.
World Pipe Band Championships, mid-Aug.
Inveraray
Highland Games, mid-Jul.
Machrihanish
Surf Rodeo, mid-Aug.
Oban
Kilmore and Kilbride Highland Games, mid-Jun.
Argyllshire Highland Gathering, late Aug.
Taynuilt
Taynuilt Highland Games, late Jul.
Tobermory, Mull
Mull Music Fest, mid-Apr.
Tour of Mull Car Rally, mid-Oct.

149

The Coach House Coffee Shop

Loch Lomond Trading Co Ltd,
Luss, G83 8NN
Tel: 01436 860341
www.lochlomondtrading.com

Gaelic music, log fires and a kilted proprietor set the scene at this friendly coffee and gift shop in the pretty village of Luss, on Loch Lomond's western shore. The perfect spot for a light meal or tea stop, it offers home-made rolls and soup, and speciality fruit cake baked with ale and studded with crystallised ginger.

Kilcamb Lodge Hotel

Strontian, Highlands PH36 4HY
Tel: 01967 402257
www.kilcamblodge.co.uk

If you're looking for a place to stop on the Ardnamurchan Peninsula, then seek out this fabulous and friendly, 300 year-old stone-built hotel just outside the village of Strontian. Basic afternoon tea includes mouthwatering home-baked shortbread, possibly flavoured with hazelnuts or orange, while a full afternoon treat includes sandwiches, cake and scones with jam and cream. Here, the main restaurant has a great reputation, too.

The Willow Tea Rooms

217 Sauchiehall Street,
Glasgow, G2 3EX
Tel: 0141 332 0521
www.willowtearooms.co.uk

Above a jewellery shop, this is one of Kate Cranston's original tea rooms designed by famous Charles Rennie Mackintosh in 1903. Sip your tea or coffee and tuck into delicious cakes, sandwiches and scones in the elegant surroundings of the Room de Luxe, with its wall-panelling, stylish stained glass and distinctive silver chairs.

KILCHURN CASTLE, LOCH AWE

LOCH LOMOND

Cairnbaan Hotel & Restaurant
Cairnbaan, by Lochgilphead, PA31 8SJ
Tel: 01546 603668

At this former 18th-century coaching inn, lighter meals are served in the lounge bar and conservatory, with lots of seafood but other choices too, such as chicken stuffed with haggis.

Crinan Hotel
Crinan, Argyll & Bute, PA31 8SR
Tel: 01546 830261
www.crinanhotel.com

The hotel is set by the little harbour, basin and lock at the end of the Crinan Canal, and offers the choice of the bar or restaurant. In both the seafood is excellent, offering such delights as a warm tart of local scallops with smoked bacon and juicy sun-dried tomatoes, or perhaps delicious West Coast mackerel.

Kilberry Inn
Kilberry, Argyll & Bute, PA29 6YD
Tel: 01880 770223

This is a little haven of comfort and good food. The building is a low stone-built farmhouse, and food served here, including the bread and chutneys, is home-made. Try a warm goat's cheese salad, or perhaps pork in prune and Armagnac sauce, or venison and game pie. Bottled beers include Arran Blonde and Fyne Ales Maverick.

Pierhouse Hotel & Restaurant
Port Appin, Argyll & Bute, PA38 4DE
Tel: 01631 730302

A whitewashed hotel, with views towards Mull, that pays tribute to the skills of local fishermen, serving simply prepared fresh lobster, bay prawns, scallops and salmon. There is an extensive wine list to match. Alternatives are chicken, venison and beef dishes, and food is served outdoors on sunny days.

LOCH GARTEN

Cairngorms & Central Highlands

AVIEMORE

BOAT OF GARTEN

BRAEMAR & DEESIDE

CAIRNGORMS NATIONAL PARK

CULLODEN

FORRES

KINGUSSIE

SPEYSIDE

INTRODUCTION

The central Highlands includes some of the highest ground in Britain: the Cairngorm mountains, where its special ecological status is protected as a national park. Two of Scotland's greatest salmon rivers flow through here too, the mighty Spey and the Dee, and this has long been a popular sporting area. Now, outdoor activities are focused around Aviemore and the Spey valley. Shaped by thousands of years of glacial ice, this brooding landscape is home to some of Scotland's most stunning birds, including golden eagles and unusual capercaillies that forage amid clumps of ancient woodland.

RIVER DEE

HOT SPOTS

Unmissable attractions

Attend the Braemar Gathering, the most famous Highland games in the world, to see, among others, tossing the caber and throwing the hammer competitions...tread the haunting ground where Bonnie Prince Charlie took on the might of the English army in the bloody Battle of Culloden...drive through the wooded Highland Wildlife Park where you can see herds of red deer and even bison from the comfort of your car...ski or snowboard down the snow-clad slopes at Aviemore, Scotlands premier winter sports venue...visit Forres, a place of condemned witches and fairy legends.

1 **Craigellachie Bridge**
Thomas Telford built this bridge over the Spey near Elgin in 1814.

2 **Strathspey Steam Railway**
The railway is based at Aviemore in the Highlands.

3 **Crathes Castle gardens**
The well-maintained castle is surrounded by wonderful gardens.

HOT SPOTS

THE BATTLE OF CULLODEN WAS FOUGHT ON THIS MOOR 16TH APRIL 1746.

THE GRAVES OF THE GALLANT HIGHLANDERS WHO FOUGHT FOR SCOTLAND & PRINCE CHARLIE ARE MARKED BY THE NAMES OF THEIR CLANS

4

5 Ruthven Barracks
The barracks were built south of Kingussie to subdue Jacobite rebellion.

6 The Cairngorms
Hikers enjoy the largest mountainscape in Britain.

5

4 Culloden Moor
A memorial to the brave Highlanders who fell in the fierce battle here.

AVIEMORE

AVIEMORE

The once-sleepy, remote railway station settlement of Aviemore was developed in the 1960s as a ski destination, and while it has never been able to rival the brash attractions of the Continental resorts, it manages to hold its own as an activities centre for the Cairngorms National Park. Its arcaded main street is a hang-over from an earlier time, but there is now a good range of outdoor shops and places to eat and relax.

The Rothiemurchus Estate, 1.5 miles (2.5km) to the south, has belonged to the Grant family since the 16th century. Elizabeth Grant's very readable account of her early life there, *Memoirs of a Highland Lady*, gives a captivating insight into the workings of the land here some 200 years ago, when timber was sawn by hand and floated down the Spey, and the idea of sustainable forestry was in barely its infancy. Today the estate offers an amazing variety of outdoor pursuits in the

Visit

SANTA'S HELPERS

This area of ancient forest is associated with rare native creatures such as wildcats, red squirrels, pine martens and capercaillies. Since the 1950s, however, its also been home to a herd of handsome, horned interlopers originating in Sweden: reindeer. Visit them at the Cairngorm Reindeer Centre in Glenmore Forest Park, where they graze on the hillside.

beautiful setting of mountains, lochs and Caledonian pine forest. This is the remains of the Old Wood of Caledon which once covered the whole country, harbouring wolves and bears, but long since was cleared for timber, fuel and farmland. Try your hand at anything from clay pigeon shooting to off-road driving, or more peaceable activities of birding, cycling, fishing and horse trekking. Don't miss the local cheeses and estate venison in the farm shop.

To the south, a good walk lasting about 1.5 hours leads around lovely Loch an Eilean, with its picturesque remains of a 15th-century castle.

Loch Morlich, 7 miles (12km) east of Aviemore, is perfect for water-based activities including sailing, windsurfing and canoeing. There is a very popular camping site, and Glenmore Lodge is a training centre for mountaineers.

To the north of Aviemore, at Carrbridge, the Landmark Highland Heritage theme park has displays on local history and wildlife as well as a treetop walk, adventure playgrounds, a maze and water slides.

BOAT OF GARTEN

Boat of Garten is an attractive little Victorian village on the west bank of the River Spey, between Aviemore and Grantown, and gets its name from the ferry that once operated here (replaced by a more convenient bridge in 1898). It is a key stop on the now preserved and restored Strathspey Steam Railway, and its station was once the point where Highland and Great North of Scotland railway companies swapped trains. The railway currently runs from Aviemore all the way to the little country station at Broomhill, which found unlikely fame as 'Glenbogle' station in the TV series, *Monarch of the Glen*. The town also has a challenging golf course, which has been described by some in the golf fraternity as a miniature version of Gleneagles.

Two miles (3km) to the east lie the still waters of Loch Garten, in the Abernethy Forest, where ospreys have nested since 1959. The RSPB has a hide there, overlooking the distant nesting site, and from where you can watch the activities of the birds in intriguing close up via a video-link. There are walking trails all through the woods around the loch. Abernethy, a national nature reserve, is the biggest Scots pine forest remaining in Britain and home to other birds such as crested tits, crossbills and capercaillies.

TICKET OFFICE
AND
RAILWAY SHOP

BOAT OF GARTEN

BALMORAL

BRAEMAR

Just to the north, the resort village of Nethy Bridge is set amid heather clad hills and native woodland, with the ruins of 13th-century Castle Roy close by and visible from the road. The walls stand up to 25 feet (7.6m) high.

Northeast of Boat of Garten, off the A95, lies the pretty little village of Dulnain Bridge. Its chief attraction is the Speyside Heather Garden and Visitor Centre at Skye of Curr, where you can purchase display heathers. There is also a garden centre, an antique shop, an art gallery, and an interesting restaurant dedicated to the Clootie Dumpling.

BRAEMAR & DEESIDE

When, in 1852, Queen Victoria and her consort Prince Albert picked an estate between Ballater and Braemar on which to build their holiday home, the entire Dee Valley acquired a cachet which it has never quite lost. Members of the royal family still spend their summer holidays at Balmoral, enjoying sports

Insight

CLOOTIE DUMPLING

The Clootie Dumpling is a suet pudding, or dumpling, traditionally wrapped and boiled in a cloth – the word 'clout' is the broad Scots for a cloth. The puddings are usually sweetened, and contain some raisins and currants, orange peel and spices, and are particularly associated with Hogmany, or New Year. The dumplings can be served boiled, or the cooled pudding can be sliced and the wedges fried in butter.

in the hills and forests, and the Braemar Gathering in September is the most famous Highland games of them all, predating Victoria's arrival by some 20 years.

Braemar itself is a bustling place, spread over the banks of the Cluny Burn. Braemar Castle lies to the east, an L-plan tower house, converted to a star-fort and barracks in the mid-18th century to guard an important military road. It is privately owned, and closed to visitors.

To the west, a narrow road leads upstream to the Linn of Dee, where the river plunges down between polished rocks into foaming pools. This is part of the 72,598-acre (29,380ha) Mar Lodge Estate, managed by the National Trust for Scotland. There are signposted walks. The road ends near a local beauty spot, the Earl of Mar's Punchbowl, where, it is said, the Earl brewed punch in a natural bowl in the rocks before the Jacobite uprising of 1715. A taxing long-distance walk from here heads into the Lairig Ghru pass to Speyside.

From Braemar the A93 follows the meandering of the river as it flows for 60 miles (96km) to the coast at Aberdeen. Ballater is a small granite-built spa town, once the terminus of a railway branch line. This is celebrated at the Old Royal Station, now an information centre which recalls the days when famous guests would alight here on their way to Balmoral. It also has some interesting little shops and an excellent tea room. To the east lies Glen Tanar, with birch woods at the Muir of Dinnet, and superb walking over the Grampian hills to the Glens of Angus.

CAIRNGORMS NATIONAL PARK

In 2003 the Cairngorms were designated Scotland's second national park, which covers a wide area of upland to the east of, and including, the Spey Valley. Over to the south the boundary continues from Dalwhinnie right across to the Glens of Angus, taking in Glen Esk before turning north to pass east of Ballater and up to Glenlivet. The centre of the national park is made up of the high granite plateaux of the Cairngorm mountains, riven by steep sided glens and deep corries, creating a sub-Arctic environment that is unique in Britain. About half the area of the park has been cleared of trees over the centuries, and is now open heather moorland, managed for grouse shooting. Around the margins, ancient areas

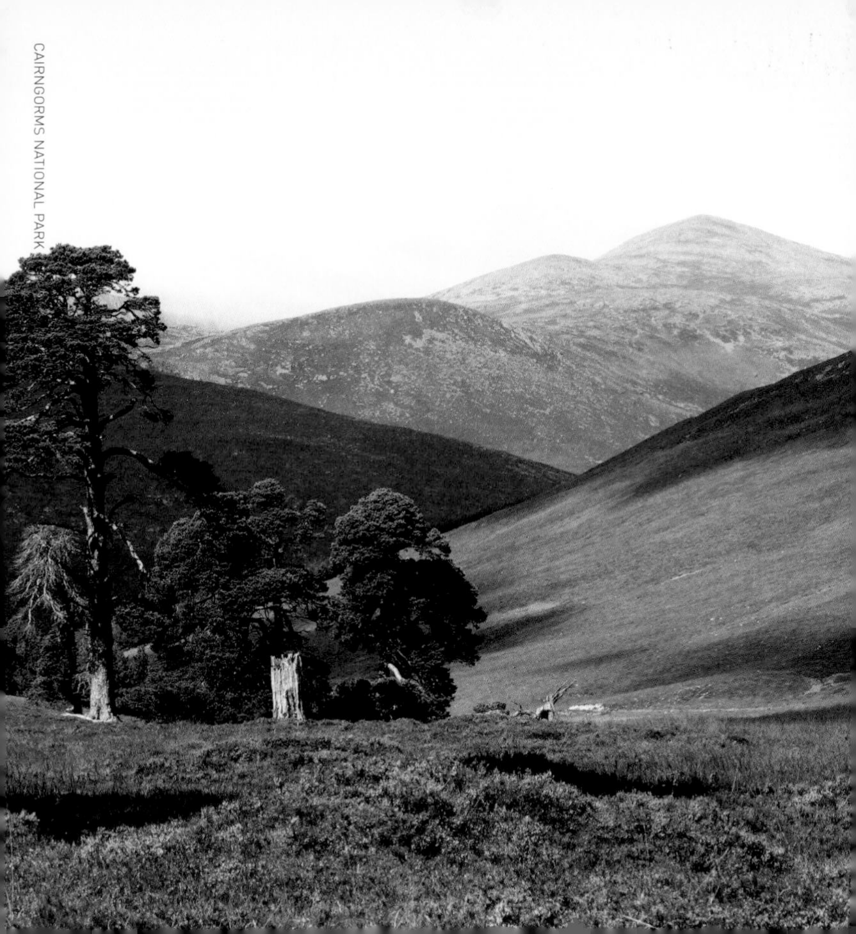

of native woodland survive, the original forests have been felled and replanted for their timber many times. The park takes in two great river valleys, the Spey and the Dee, and it is along these that most of its small population of about 14,000 live and work, their numbers swelled in summer by visitors looking for outdoor adventure, and in winter by snow-sports enthusiasts.

There's an extensive network of paths in the glens and forests around the Cairngorms, from starting points such as Nethy Bridge, Rothiemurchus, Aviemore, Glenmore, Grantown-on Spey, Tomintoul, Ballater, Braemar and glens Tanar, Doll and Feshie. More experience is needed to tackle the heights such as Ben Macdhui, Cairn Gorm and Cairn Toul. There are plenty of great opportunities for cycling, fishing and golf, and watersports are focused on Loch Insh and Loch Morlich. There are ski centres at Cairngorm, the Lecht and Glenshee, and a funicular railway

Insight

LICHENS

You will see plenty of healthy lichens in the Cairngorms. Lichens are very sensitive to pollution and don't grow in places where the air is contaminated and they are a sign that the air is particularly clear and clean.

runs to the summit of Cairngorm (there is no access beyond the summit station during the summer).

Signs of the earliest settlers may be seen in the hummocks of hill forts such as Dun da lamh, near Laggan, and the mound of a crannog on Loch Kinnord. Queen Victoria was enchanted by this romantic landscape and built her holiday home, Balmoral Castle, at Braemar in 1853, popularising the region and also beginning a royal connection that still holds to this day. One of the oddest memorials associated with her is the crown-shaped monument built over a spring in remote Glen Mark, known as the Queen's Well.

173

CULLODEN

The Battle of Culloden marked the end of Stuart ambitions to reclaim the throne of Britain from the Hanoverians. On this bleak and desolate moorland east of Inverness, 5,000 Highlanders under the command of the Young Pretender – Bonnie Prince Charlie – faced 9,000 troops led by the Duke of Cumberland. It was 16th April 1746, a day of bitter cold, with snow flurries. The Highlanders, used to short skirmishes, were no match for the disciplined and well-armed soldiers, and despite courageous fighting were swiftly defeated. Cumberland ordered that no prisoners should be taken.

Although it can be very crowded in summer, Culloden remains an evocative and moving place. The 1,200 Highlanders who died were buried in clan graves, marked by small, weathered stones. The 76 English dead soldiers lie in the Field of the English. Coloured flags fly over the battlefield to mark the position of the armies, and the focal point of the area is a large 19th-century memorial cairn, built where the fighting was most ferocious.

The Visitor Centre has clear explanations of the battle, its causes and its aftermath. Prince Charles fled to the hills and eventually escaped to France. The clans were ruthlessly suppressed – the kilt, tartan, the Gaelic language and even the bagpipes were proscribed.

FORRES

The ancient market town of Forres, on the River Findhorn, was once plagued by witches. William Shakespeare made full use of this in *Macbeth* (c1606), when he set scenes with the three 'weird sisters' in the area. Three more witches, burned to death, are commemorated with an iron-bound stone in the town. Forres' importance, hinted at in some of its grander buildings, was eclipsed by that of Elgin in the 13th century. Sueno's Stone, on the eastern outskirts, is a Pictish

cross-slab which stands 20 feet (6m) tall and is believed to date from the 9th or 10th centuries. The sandstone is intricately carved in five sections with vivid scenes from an unidentified and bloody battle, and is now protected from the elements by a huge glass box. Southeast of the town, Cluny Hill is the highest point, topped by an octagonal tower, raised in 1806 to commemorate Lord Nelson. It is believed to be the first such monument in Britain, and provides a magnificent viewpoint. To the south of Forres, the Dallas Dhu Historic Distillery is preserved by Historic Scotland.

Remarkably, Pluscarden Abbey is the only medieval foundation in Britain still used for its original purpose. To the east of Forres, the monastery is the home of 27 Benedictine monks, and a haven of spiritual retreat for both men and women. The monastery was founded in 1230 by Alexander II, and during the Reformation in the 16th century was gradually abandoned.

In 1943 Benedictine monks began its restoration and in 1974 it was granted abbey status. Today the white-habited monks work in the grounds and workshops and care for the abbey buildings. These centre on the massive abbey church, where ancient stonework and frescoes contrast with modern stained glass.

KINGUSSIE

The little town of Kingussie lies in the beautiful Spey Valley, once the capital of the ancient area of Badenoch, and with a history that dates back to pre-Pictish times. Today it is best known as home to the Highland Folk Museum, a place with fascinating indoor and outdoor exhibits. In fact, the museum occupies two sites, the other being situated at Newtonmore, to the south. The main house here contains traditional furniture and bygones, and a representation of a Highland kitchen; in the grounds you will find a reconstructed Hebridean mill, a salmon smokehouse in addition to a primitive blackhouse from Lewis. There are regular craft demonstrations and participation during the summer.

Half a mile ((800m) southeast of Kingussie are the impressive Ruthven Barracks, dramatically set on a grassy mound, formerly the site of a castle, and built in 1718 in order to subdue the Highlands, following the 1715 Jacobite rebellion. Despite being set on fire by the fleeing Jacobite army in 1746, there are still considerable remains. The garrison here guarded General Wade's military road, leading from Glen Truim in the south.

The adjacent Insh Marshes Reserve (RSPB), an important site for breeding waders and wintering waterfowl, has hides and nature trails. There is also a guided tour. You can walk from here to beautiful Glen Tromie.

Just to the north of Kingussie, off the B9152, is the noted Highland Wildlife Park, an extensive reserve and exhibition of themed habitats dedicated to Scottish wildlife, and part of the Royal Zoological Society of Scotland (the owners of Edinburgh Zoo). A driving tour takes in herds of red deer, as well as ancient breeds of bison and horse, before you explore the rest on foot. Look out for otters, owls, boars, Arctic foxes, wildcat and eagles. You can also follow, in your car, the vehicle that delivers a feed at 10am each day, or take a guided tour in the morning or afternoon. The centre is perhaps best known for its wolves, and a raised walkway takes visitors safely into the heart of their (well-fenced) enclosure. The last wild wolf in Scotland was killed in 1743.

The nearby village of Kincraig is the access point for Loch Insh, popular for watersports, and its ski school has a dry ski slope (200ft/ 60m). A church on the loch shore reputedly stands on a site where worship has been continuous since the 6th century.

Kingussie is just 12 miles (20km) from Aviemore ski resort.

SPEYSIDE

The Spey is one of the foremost salmon rivers in Scotland, flowing northeast from its source on Craig a' Cleat, in the Monadhliath Mountains along a broad strath, or valley, finally reaching the sea at Spey Bay, to the west of Buckie. Although it starts in the mountainous Highlands, its lower reaches are more characteristic of lowland scenery. Along its course, it is fed by crystal-clear, fresh streams from high in the Cairngorms, including the Feshie and the Nethy.

The river itself is unnavigable by craft, but the Speyside Way long-distance footpath follows its route for 84 miles (135km) from the police station at Aviemore to the coast, passing Grantown-on-Spey, Cromdale and the Craigellachie Forest, with spur paths joining from Tomintoul and Dufftown.

The Spey Valley is equally renowned for the quality of its malt whisky – you'll not have to travel far without spotting the distinctive

Visit

THE COOPER'S CRAFT

None of the distilleries of Strathspey could thrive without the specially crafted wooden barrels or casks in which the spirit is left to mature. For an insight into the cooper's skill, you can visit the family-run, fully working Speyside Cooperage just south of Craigellachie. Oak for the barrel staves is largely imported from the USA, and the cooperage produces around 100,000 casks a year for shipping around the world – oak is preferred for its qualities of 'breathing'.

pointed chimney-caps of a distillery, for there are more than 30 along the river and its tributaries. Pick up the official 75-mile (120km) Malt Whisky Trail for a tour of some of Scotland's finest. Distilleries that welcome visitors include Glenfiddich, founded by William Grant in 1887 at Dufftown, and the Aberlour Distillery (Walkers Shortbread is also made in Aberlour. There is also a factory shop).

Visit

EARLY CAIRNS

If you think archaeological sites are a bit dull, visit the fascinating Clava Cairns near Culloden, which opens a window on how our remote ancestors lived four thousand years ago.

A site of major archaeological importance, and very beautifully set among superb beech trees, the site has three large stone burial mounds, each surrounded by a circle of standing stones. They were probably built between about 2000 and 1500 BC.

The two outer cairns, still partly covered in small boulders, have stone-lined passages to the centre. The northeast cairn has an interesting series of cup marks on one of the larger boulders. The middle one is hollow, though with no passage. Instead, it has rough cobbled pavements leading away from it.

Clava Cairns is part of a whole series of such monuments found only in the region of the Moray Firth.

Grantown-on-Spey is one of the largest settlements along the river bank. The town was planned out in 1765, and has a spacious, genteel feel to it today. Its creator James Grant returned from his Grand Tour of Europe in 1750. He'd seen Edinburgh New Town , just then being built, and thought Speyside could do with something similar.

The arrival of the railway in 1863 heralded the town's popularity as a health resort. The railway folded in the 1960s, and the town is now better known as a centre for anglers, and walkers. Its story is told in the local museum.

The upper reaches of the Spey, between Loch Laggan and Grantown-on-Spey, made the perfect backdrop for the popular TV series, *Monarch of the Glen*. Laggan village doubled as 'Glenbogle', and the Victorian mansion of Ardverikie (private) on its shores provided the main setting. Location hunters should check the leaflet *Monarch of the Glen Country*.

PLACES OF INTEREST

Aberlour Distillery
High Street, Aberlour
Tel: 01340 881249

Balmoral Castle
Ballater.
Tel: 013397 42534;
www.balmoralcastle.com

Cairngorm Mountain Railway
Cairngorm Ski Area, by Aviemore.
Tel: 01479 861261;
www.cairngormmountain.org

Corgarff Castle
Strathdon.
Tel: 019756 51460

Dallas Dhu Historic Distillery
Mannachie Road, Forres.
Tel: 01309 676548

Dalwhinnie Distillery
Dalwhinnie,
www.newtonmore.com/dalwhinnie

Elgin Cathedral
King Street, Elgin.
Tel: 01343 547171

Findhorn Community
The Park, Findhorn
Tel: 01309 690311;
www.findhorn.org

Glenfiddich Distillery
Dufftown
Tel: 01340 820373;
www.glenfiddich.com

Glenlivet Distillery
Ballindalloch
Tel: 01340 821720;
www.theglenlivet.com

Grantown Museum
Burnfield Avenue,
Grantown-on-Spey
Tel: 01479 872478

Highland Folk Museum
Duke Street, Kingussie.
Tel: 01540 661307;
www.highlandfolk.com

Loch Garten Osprey Centre
By Boat of Garten.
Tel: 01479 821894;
www.rspb.org.uk

Mar Lodge Estate
Braemar.
Tel: 013397 41433;
www.marlodgeestate.org.uk

Moray Firth Wildlife Centre
Tugnet, Spey Bay.
Tel: 01343 820339;
www.wdcs.org/wildlifecentre

Old Royal Station
Station Square, Ballater.
Tel: 013397 55306;
www.aberdeen-grampian.com

Pluscarden Abbey
Pluscarden, Elgin.
Tel: 01343 890257;
www.pluscardenabbey.org

Royal Lochnagar Distillery
Crathie, Ballater.
Tel: 013397 42700;
www.malts.com

Speyside Cooperage
Dufftown Road, Craigellachie.
Tel: 01340 871108;
www.speysidecooperage.co.uk

Speyside Heather Garden and Visitor Centre
Skye of Curr, Dulnain Bridge.
Tel: 01479 851359;
www.heathercentre.com

Strathspey Steam Railway
Aviemore, Boat of Garten.
Tel: 01479 810725;
www.strathspeyrailway.co.uk

FOR CHILDREN

Cairngorm Reindeer Centre
Reindeer House, Glenmore.
Tel: 01479 861228;
www.reindeercompany.demon.co.uk

Highland Wildlife Park
Kincraig, by Kingussie.
Tel: 01540 651270;
www.highlandwildlifepark.org

Landmark Highland Heritage Park
Carrbridge. Tel: 01479 841613;
www.landmark-centre.co.uk

SPORTS & ACTIVITIES

ADVENTURE SPORTS

Absolute Full On Adventure
24 Cairngorm Avenue, Aviemore.
Tel: 07885 835838;
www.fullonadventure.com

Active Outdoor Pursuits
Craigower Lodge Outdoor Centre,
Golf Course Road, Newtonmore.
Tel: 08450 505052;
www.activeoutdoorpursuits.com

Glenmore Lodge
By Aviemore.
Tel: 01479 861256;
www.glenmorelodge.org.uk

Rothiemurchus Estate
By Aviemore. Tel: 01479 812345;
www.rothiemurchus.net

CYCLING

Cycle Highlands
The Pavilion, Victoria Road, Ballater.
Tel: 013397 55864;
www.cyclehighlands.com

FISHING

Fishdee Ltd
Estate Office, Dinnet, Aboyne.
Tel: 01573 470612; www.fishdee.co.uk

Glen Tanar Estate
Brooks House, Glen Tanar, Aboyne.
Tel: 013398 86451;
www.glentanar.co.uk

GOLF

Abernethy Golf Club
Nethybridge.
www.abernethygolfclub.com

Grantown-on-Spey Golf Club
Golf Course Road.
Tel: 01479 872079;
www.grantownonspeygolfclub.co.uk

Kingussie Golf Club
Gynack Road, Kingussie.
Tel: 01540 661600;
www.kingussie-golf.co.uk

HORSE-RIDING

Glen Tanar Equestrian Centre
Glen Tanar, Aboynes. Tel: 013398 86448

Tomintoul Riding Centre
St Bridget Farm, Tomintoul.
Tel: 01807 580210

LONG-DISTANCE PATHS

Speyside Way
Aviemore to Buckie, 84 miles (135km).
www.speysideway.org

WATERSPORTS

**Loch Insh Watersports/
Insh Hall Ski School**
Kincraig. Tel: 01540 651272;
www.lochinsh.com

Loch Morlich Watersports Centre
Glenmore Forest Park, by Aviemore.
Tel: 01479 861221;
www.lochmorlich.com

WILDLIFE TOURS

Speyside Wildlife
Rothiemurchus Visitor Centre,
by Aviemore. Tel: 01479 812498;
www.speysidewildlife.co.uk

WINTER SPORTS

Aviemore Ski & Snowboard Hire
131 Grampian Road.
Tel: 01479 811711; www.osatravel.co.uk

Glenshee Ski Centre
Cairnwell, by Braemar.
Tel: 013397 41320;
www.ski-glenshee.co.uk
Insh Hall Ski School
Kincraig.Tel: 01540 651272;
www.lochinsh.com
Lecht 2090 Ski and Multi-Activity Centre
Strathdon, on A939.
Tel: 01975 651440; www.lecht.co.uk

SHOPPING
A'Anside Studios
5 Main Street, Tomintoul.
Tel: 01479 872074;
www.aanside.co.uk
Scottish arts and crafts.
Baxters Highland Village
Fochabers, on the A96.
Tel: 01343 820666;
www.baxters.com
Shops at the soup factory.
Ellis Brigham
9–10 Grampian Road, Aviemore.
Tel: 01479 810175;
www.ellis-brigham.com
Outdoor sports gear.

Johnston's of Elgin Cashmere Visitor Centre
Newmill, Elgin.Tel: 01343 554099;
www.johnstonscashmere.com
Lamont Sporrans Ltd
8 Invercauld Road, Braemar.
Tel: 013397 41404;
www.lamontsporrans.co.uk
Full range of kilts and Highland dress.

ANNUAL EVENTS & CUSTOMS
Abernethy
Highland Games, Aug.
Aviemore
Highland Feast – Scottish food and drink festival, end Sep to Oct.
Braemar
Braemar Gathering, early Sep.
Carrbridge
World Porridge Making Championships, early Oct.
Grantown-on-Spey
Highland Games, end Aug.
Rothiemurchus/Aviemore
Highland Games World Cup, early Aug.
Speyside
Sprit of Speyside Whisky Festival, end Apr to May.

TEA ROOMS

Brodie Countryfare
Brodie, by Forres, Morayshire,
IV36 2TD
Tel: 01309 641555
www.brodiecountryfare.com
On the A96 close to Brodie Castle,
this busy shopping complex offers a
foodhall and good delicatessen full
of rich aromas. Only the best local
ingredients are served up in the
restaurant, whether it's freshly baked
scones with your cup of tea or a more
substantial meal.

The Clootie Dumpling
Speyside Heather Garden & Visitor
Centre, Skye of Curr, Dulnain Bridge,
Highland, PH26 3PA
Tel: 01479 851359
www.heathercentre.com
Tea, coffee, sandwiches, speciality
soups and other traditional home-
made foods are available all day – but
the highlight has got to be the Clootie
Dumpling, which is served in 21
different ways.

Culloden Visitor Centre
Culloden Moor, Inverness,
Highland, IV2 5EU
Tel: 01463 790607
The lovely café/restaurant here serves
light lunches and snacks, including
vegetable soups complimented by
freshly baked cheese scones.

The Victorian Station
Coffee Shop
Station Square, Ballater, AB35 5QB
Tel: 07840 745313
Complete your day's visit to the
handsomely restored Old Royal Station
by tucking into some home-baking
at this excellent café, with its good
Italian-style coffees. Freshly made food
includes soups, toasties and paninis.

Cawdor Tavern

The Lane, Cawdor, Highland, IV12 5PX
Tel: 01667 404777

Close to the famous castle, this pub
is in a former estate building. The pub
has an excellent reputation for its food,
offering main courses such as battered
fillet of sea bream, and chicken stuffed
with haggis. There are good children's
facilities, and dogs are allowed. Beers
include Tomintoul Stag.

Gordon Arms Hotel

80 High Street, Fochabers, IV32 7DH
Tel: 01343 820508
www.gordonarmshotel.com

This popular 200-year-old former
coaching inn is close to some of
Speyside's best distilleries. It serves
local produce, including seafood from
the Moray coast, salmon from the
Spey river close by, and venison and
lamb from the uplands. The choice
of beers here includes brews such
as Caledonian Deuchars IPA, John
Smith's Smooth, Scottish Courage and
Marsdons Pedigree.

The Old Bridge Inn

Dalfaber Road, Aviemore,
Highland, PH22 1PU
Tel: 01479 810270

A cosy, friendly Highland pub
overlooking the River Spey, with an
attractive riverside garden as a bonus
for high summer. Bar meals include
lamb chops with redcurrant jelly,
Aberdeen Angus steaks, or perhaps
chicken breast marinated in lime,
yoghurt and coriander. There's also a
large selection of fine malt whiskies to
sample, if you so desire.

Tipsy Laird

68 High Street, Kingussie,
Highland, PH21 1HZ
Tel: 01540 661334
www.thetipsylaird.co.uk

Look out for tasty venison burgers,
freshly prepared soup, and sandwiches
or grilled panini on the light lunch
menu at this popular walkers' and
outdoor enthusiasts' pub in Kingussie.
Hostel-style accommodation is also
available here.

BEN NEVIS

Skye & Northern Highlands

APPLECROSS	**INVERNESS**
BLACK ISLE	**INVERPOLLY**
CANNICH	**LOCH NESS**
FORT WILLIAM	**MALLAIG**
GAIRLOCH	**SHIELDAIG & TORRIDON**
GLENELG	**SKYE**
GLENFINNAN	**STRATHPEFFER**
INVEREWE	**ULLAPOOL**

INTRODUCTION

Northern Scotland contains some of the country's most dramatic features, from the slash of the Great Glen and mystical Loch Ness, Britain's deepest freshwater lake, to Ben Nevis, its highest mountain. As the landscapes are bigger and the climate harsher, so the population is sparser. Exceptions are found on the west coast, where a fabulous garden flourishes in the comparative warmth at Inverewe. Wildlife watching is a key attraction, with otters, dolphins, seals, and occasionally whales.

LOCH NESS

HOT SPOTS

Unmissable attractions

Ride to the top of the Nevis Range for stunning views of the craggy mountains and deep lochs below...visit the Museum and Art Gallery at Inverewe where you can learn about the geological and historical make-up of the area or wander through the impressive gardens established here by Osgood MacKenzie...marvel at the superb engineering mastery of the Caledonian Canal and its complex series of lochs...climb aboard the Western Line railway, one of the most scenic journeys in Britain...stand on the shore of Loch Ness and summon the legendary monster to appear...join a whale-watching cruise off the coast from Fort William or scan the ocean for friendly bottlenose dolphins...explore the romantic Isle of Skye.

1

1 Rhum
The view towards Rhum, a superb National Nature Reserve and home to Kinloch Castle.

2 Inverness Castle
This 19th-century castle was built on the site of an 11th-century castle which was destroyed in 1746.

3 Inverewe Garden
Osgood Mackenzie's vision in the 19th century resulted in the stunning gardens on a steep rocky promontory near Loch Ewe.

4 Isle of Skye
Pony-trekking is a leisurely way to see the wonderful Isle of Skye.

5 Caledonian Canal
Boats moored at Fort Augustus on the canal.

6 Glenfinnan Valley
The Jacobite steam train puffs gently through the Glenfinnan Valley where it stops at Mallaig.

4

5

6

APPLECROSS

Looking north from pretty Plockton, the rugged hills of Applecross fill both the view and the imagination. Until the last century this peninsula was almost as isolated as Knoydart. Rough tracks linked the old settlements along the coast down to Toscaig, and access up from the south was via the breathtaking Bealach-na-Ba pass, which rises to some 2,050 feet (624.8m). In 1965 a road was started around the northern margin from Shieldaig, making it a pleasant circular drive.

An Irish saint established a religious community here in the 7th century, but it was destroyed in a Viking raid. Today it is hard to believe that 3,000 people once thrived with their cattle in the fertile valley around the quiet village of Applecross – cleared from the land when the Mackenzies sold it off for a sporting estate; only the outlines of their deserted cottages remain.

Applecross Bay is a welcoming curve of pinkish sand, with a little inn noted for its fresh seafood.

BLACK ISLE

This the fertile spit of land between the Cromarty and Moray Firths. The central forested ridge carries the peninsula's older name of Ardmeanach, and was part of lands gifted by Mary, Queen of Scots to her husband (and cousin), Lord Darnley.

Visit

EILEAN DONAN CASTLE

One of the most photographed and romantic castles in Scotland, Eilean Donan is perched on a rock just offshore in Loch Duich, linked to the mainland and a modern visitor centre by a stone bridge. There's been a fortification here since the 13th century and its 14-foot (4.26m) thick walls have withstood the onslaught of both men and the elements. The castle owes its appearance today to restoration between 1912 and 1932, by Lt Col John MacRae-Gilstrap, who had a vision in a dream of how it should look.

EILEAN DONAN CASTLE

Cromarty, set on the northeastern tip of the peninsula, is an fine 18th-century town, and an important centre of fishing and commerce until the 19th century, when it was bypassed by the railways. The whitewashed Courthouse Museum tells the town's story, with the aid of computer-controlled, animated figures. Hugh Miller, a 19th-century geologist, social commentator and also writer, lived in the little thatched cottage next door. The cottage is now in the care of the National Trust for Scotland. The interesting fossil beach where he worked is 2 miles (3.2 km) away at Eathie.

Fortrose looks out across the lovely Moray Firth. The cathedral was completed in the 15th century, but was then unroofed in the 16th century, before Cromwell plundered its great sandstone blocks to build the fortifications in Inverness. On the other side of the spit (once a popular spot for witch-burning but now dedicated to golf) lies Rosemarkie, notable for the fascinating Pictish remains displayed at the Groam House Museum and Pictish Centre, which is worth a visit.

The mudflats of the Beauly Firth attract a large number of birds – over-wintering greylag and pink-footed geese graze the fields around, and a variety of sea ducks, including goldeneye and scoter, may be spotted near the Kessock Bridge.

In the graveyard of the parish church of Avoch, near Rosemarkie, lie the remains of the great Scottish explorer Sir Alexander Mackenzie (1755–1820). Mackenzie travelled to Canada in 1779 and was soon trading furs for the North West Company. Based at Fort Chipewyan on Lake Athabasca, he set out with a team of native Canadian Indians in 1789 to discover a route across the continent, but found instead a long river, which would be named after him, leading up to the Arctic Ocean. In 1793 he became the first white man to cross the Rockies and reach the Pacific.

CANNICH

The broad Strath Glass from the north leads to the modern village of Cannich where four valleys meet. Eastwards, down Glen Urquhart, is the prehistoric Corrimony Cairn, still with its stone roof and eleven standing stones. Dramatic Glen Cannich is entered by a winding road between bare mountain tops, with groves of birch and alder. It widens towards Loch Mullardoch and its dam, 9 miles (15km) west of Cannich, at 2,385 feet (726.5m), is the longest in Scotland.

The approach to Glen Affric, perhaps the most beautiful of Scottish valleys, passes the popular Dog Falls. Along this 6 mile (9.7km) stretch of Loch Beinn a'Mheadhoin are parking spots, many with fine walks starting from them. On the opposite side is one of the largest remnants of the ancient Caledonian Pine Forest, fenced to keep out deer and allow regeneration. Beyond the loch the road ends, but you can walk on to Loch Affric – a magical scene

Activity

DOLPHIN WATCH

Bottlenose dolphins found around the Scottish mainland are some of the largest in the world, and in the Moray Firth area there is currently one of only two resident populations in Britain, with at least 88 individuals identified. Cromarty has become the best place in Britain to see bottlenose dolphins in the wild – boat trips run by Dolphin Ecosse are available throughout the year. There are also whale-watching trips in August and September.

of clustered hills, birch and pine forest; during the autumn there is dazzling colour and a hint of snow on the peaks. You can also follow the old track up through the mountains to Sheil Bridge in Kintail.

FORT WILLIAM

Fort William's greatest asset is its close proximity to Ben Nevis, Britain's highest mountain, which stands sentinel over the Nevis range

about 7 miles (11.5km) to the north. The town is also at the southern entrance to the Great Glen and at the head of Loch Linnhe, with routes to Badenoch and Skye. But this is not just a place to venture from – it has its own delights too. The idiosyncratic West Highland Museum, famous for the Jacobite collections held there, lives up to its description as 'an old-fashioned museum – it is full of information and surprises' with an eclectic range of displays, including natural history, Highland clothing and crofting. Treasures of the Earth, at Corpach to the west of town, is a huge collection of rare gemstones, crystals and fossils, including Europe's largest uncut emerald. Visitors can also discover how amethyst crystals take a quarter of a million years to grow just 1 inch (3cm).

Until recently the tops of Scotland's mountain ranges were the exclusive preserve of the athletic, but now everyone can experience breathtaking views without so much

Insight

ATTAINING THE HEIGHTS

Until well into the 19th century everyone thought that soaring Ben Macdhui in the Cairngorms, and not Ben Nevis, was Britain's highest mountain. It was the peak everyone climbed, including Gladstone and even Queen Victoria. She wrote in her journal, 'Nothing could be grander or wilder; the rocks are so grand and precipitous, and the snow on Ben Macdhui has such fine effect.' Like Everest, only recognised as the world's highest mountain in the 19th century, Ben Nevis remained unrecognised until accurate measurement was made by the Ordnance Survey in 1846 and the issue was resolved – Ben Nevis is the highest at 4,406 feet (1,343m), and Ben Macdhui is runner-up at 4,296 feet (1,309m).

as getting out of breath. Panoramic vistas to the upper slopes of Aonach Mor (4,000 ft/1,219.2m) open up from enclosed gondola cable cars which cover about 1.5 miles (2.4km)

in their climb to an altitude of 2,150 feet (655.3m). The ascent takes about 15 minutes and at the top, in addition to the breathtaking views across Loch Lochy, the Great Glen,

Loch Eil and the Inner Hebrides, you will find a restaurant, a sports shop, telescopes, interpretative plaques and slide presentations. There are a number of walks but do keep to the paths, both for your own safety and for conservation. Two recommended walks are to Sgurr Finnisg-aig (taking about 20 minutes each way) and to Meal Beag (taking about 30 minutes in each direction).

Visit

THE PARALLEL ROADS

In a quiet valley 18 miles (29km) to the northeast of Fort William is a geological phenomenon that is unique in Britain. Glen Roy and its side valleys are marked by three strange parallel lines known as the 'Parallel Roads', not roads at all, but the shorelines of an ancient glacial loch. Towards the end of the last Ice Age, abou 10,000 years ago, the valley was dammed with ice that melted in three seperated stages, leaving these horizontal ridges along the valley slopes. Scottish Natural Heritage explains it all on an interpretative board above the car park. To get to Glen Roy from Fort William, go north on the A82, turn right on to the A86 at Spean Bridge, then left on an unclassified road at Roy Bridge.

GAIRLOCH

This popular holiday village with its excellent Heritage Museum is spread around a sunny, sandy bay, with the heights of the delightfully named Flowerdale looming behind. There are superb views out to the islands, and Gairloch lies at the heart of a fine scenic area which takes in the incomparable Loch Maree. West from the village, the road winds around the bay and eventually turns into a track, leading to the former lighthouse at Rubha Reidh. To the south of the bay there are many intriguing woody inlets,

GAIRLOCH

perfect for exploring in a small boat. Beyond sheltered Badachro the road passes sandy bays to end at Redpoint, but energetic walkers can take the long path to Diabaig on Loch Torridon.

Behind Gairloch the A832 leads to the long stretch of water that is Loch Maree, famous for its fishing. It is surrounded by high mountains and scattered with darkly wooded islands. The highest peak on the northern shore is Slioch (3,219 feet/981m), while to the south Beinn Eighe, with its cap of white quartzite, lies at the heart of Britain's first National Nature Reserve. You can find out about nature trails and picnic spots at the visitor centre at Aultroy, towards the eastern end of the loch.

Isle Maree, by Letterewe, was the site of a 7th-century hermitage, and may even have had much older, druidical connections. Queen Victoria fell in love with the whole area when she visited in 1877, giving her name to the waterfall near Talladale.

GLENELG

The old military road that leads up to Glenelg rockets off the main Kyle of Lochalsh road, climbing rapidly up the Mam Ratagain pass to a fine viewpoint offering stunning views of the lovely Five Sisters of Kintail above Loch Duich. There follows a gentler descent into Glen More, where a side road goes to the six-car turntable ferry that is a summer alternative to the bridge to Skye.

The Glenelg road passes the gaunt remains of Bernera Barracks, built in 1722 for Hanoverian troops (ruins fenced off for safety reasons). Continue for 2.5 miles (4km) into Glen Beag for Glenelg's most famous sight – its two brochs.

The circular walls of Dun Telve still stand to 33 feet (10m), and are 13 feet (3.9m) wide at the base. Dun Troddan is more ruined, but in both you can still see the remains of the internal galleries and stairways.

Admirers of Gavin Maxwell's marvellous book *Ring of Bright Water* will want to go even further

Insight

SCOTS BROCHS

Only Scotland has brochs, those distinct, cooling-tower-shaped structures, built in the Iron Age, from around 500 BC to AD 100. Some 500 sites have been identified, mostly near the sea and in areas where timber was scarce but stone was plentiful. No one knows their function, but they were probably defensive – the name is from Old Norse borg, meaning a fortress. The open interiors had galleries and parapets, and elaborate internal staircases, all carefully constructed. The best-preserved is on Mousa in Shetland.

GLENFINNAN

Glenfinnan will always have a special place in Scottish history, for it was here that the event which Winston Churchill called 'one of the most audacious and irresponsible enterprises in British history' began – the 1745 Jacobite Rising. The monument tower of 1815, with its 1834 figure of a Highlander, may not be on the exact spot where Bonnie Prince Charlie unfurled his father's white and red silk banner, yet it is most romantically set at the head of Loch Shiel, overlooking the wooded Eilean Glean Fhianin and the mountains of Sunart and Moidart. Climb the tower for the best views of the loch.

The clan chiefs were dismayed that the Prince had brought only seven followers, not the French troops they had expected. They were persuaded to join him only by the example of Cameron of Lochiel, who brought 700 men to Glenfinnan for the Prince. So on 19 August 1745 the banner was set flying, the Old

along the coast to Sandaig, where the author lived and where he kept his famous otters in the 1950s. The house he called Camusfearna in his books stood near the shore of the beautiful bay, but was burned down and then demolished, at his request on his death. Maxwell's ashes lie under a boulder here, and a cairn has an inscription to Edal the otter.

Pretender was proclaimed King James III & VIII, with the Prince as his Regent, and the army – still only 1,200 strong – began its campaign. Capturing Edinburgh easily and defeating General Cope in the 15-minute battle at Prestonpans on 21 September, they set out for London. But with little English support and no hope of French help, they turned back at Derby that December and met their doom at Culloden the following April.

The story is vividly told in the Visitor Centre near by, which also traces the Prince's journeys through the Western Highlands and Islands after Culloden.

INVEREWE

Surrounded by barren peat bogs, rocks and water lies Inverewe, one of Britain's most remarkable gardens, and a must-see for plant-lovers from all over the world. Lying on the same line of latitude as Moscow and Hudson's Bay, the site must have seemed a daunting challenge

Activity

FLOWER POTS TO POT SHOTS

Osgood Mackenzie, creator of Inverewe Garden, was a typical Victorian gentlemen when it came to sport. He was a keen shot and proud of his success. In 1856 alone he records bagging 184 hares, 110 golden plover, 91 rock pigeons, 35 wild duck, 53 snipe and 49 partridges, as well as 1,313 grouse – and this does not include roe deer, ptarmigan, teal and geese.

when Osgood MacKenzie inherited the Inverewe Estate in 1862 from his step-father. Osgood possessed every skill and quality necessary in order to create this wonderful oasis – imagination, vision, perseverance and patience.

First he planted a shelter belt of pines and firs, carted out the rocks and replaced them with hundreds of tonnes of garden soil. Once protected against strong winds, Inverewe could benefit from the warming effects of the North

219

Atlantic Drift. Rhododendrons were planted in profusion, and still provide one of the most spectacular attractions in the early summer. Paths meander between the blooms and beneath the pines, and pass an almost bewildering array of rare and exotic plants, collected from all over the world. Rock gardens are bright with alpines, including many species from New Zealand, and the area named 'Japan' is planted with a variety of tree ferns and palms.

There are wonderful views along the loch from the tip of the garden at Cuddy Rock, and also from the front of the house, built in 1937 after fire destroyed Osgood's original building. Mackenzie died in 1922, and his daughter Mairi, who had maintained and developed his vision, presented the garden to the National Trust for Scotland in 1952.

Visit

A HIGHLAND WINERY

Few visitors to Scotland would expect to be able to buy locally produced wines, but that is exactly what you can do at Moniack Castle, 7 miles (11.3km) west of Inverness, near Kirkhill. But even the south-facing slopes of the Highland hills cannot support grape-vines, and it is traditional 'country wines' that you will find here – elderflower, silver birch, mead and sloe gin. This unique Highland enterprise is housed in the former fortress of the Lovat chiefs, where visitors can sample the produce in a wine bar and bistro.

INVERNESS

Inverness is known as the 'Capital of the Highlands', Scotland's newest city (designated in 2000) and a popular holiday centre, set on the banks of the River Ness at the eastern extremity of the Great Glen. Commanding the east–west facing corridor to Moray and Aberdeen as well as the main north–south route through Scotland, its location has given the town a strategic importance that has resulted in a much chequered history. Inverness was probably well established by the time of St Columba's visit in AD 565. Certainly King Duncan (c1010–1040), notably of Shakespeare's Macbeth, had his castle in the town, and various clan chiefs and disaffected Jacobites have stormed through the town over the centuries.

Today Inverness is a busy administrative centre for the Highlands and Islands and presents a mostly 19th-century face. Even the dominating red sandstone walls of Inverness Castle were rebuilt during Victoria's reign as a Sheriff Court and jail, with a monument to Flora Macdonald on the castle esplanade. On the opposite side of the river loom the two massive towers of St Andrew's Episcopal Cathedral, which contains a collection of Russian icons. The Inverness Museum and Art Gallery, has fine examples of Highland artefacts and displays on the archaeology, social and natural history of the Highlands. The museum hosts various exhibitions, performances and talks.

Insight

CONCRETE BOB'S VIADUCT

The West Highland Railway gives views down Loch Shiel from the Glenfinnan Viaduct, which is very impressive. It was built when the line from Glasgow, which had struggled across Rannoch Moor to Fort William by 1894, was extended to Mallaig in 1902. Curving over 1,000 feet (308m) over the River Finnan, its 21 concrete arches are up to 100 feet (30.5m) high. The viaduct was designed for Robert MacAlpine (later Sir Robert, founder of the civil engineering firm) whose nickname was Concrete Bob. It is said that buried within the viaduct are a horse and cart that fell into the concrete before it set.

From the museum you can see Craig Phadrig, a vitrified Iron Age fort on a wooded hill west of the River Ness, reached by a steep forest trail from Leachkin Brae. In Huntly Street next to the river you can visit the kilt-making workshop of Hector Russell's Scottish Kiltmaker.

INVERNESS

Visit

THE CURSE OF CALDA HOUSE

Near to the old ruins of the MacLeods' 15th-century Ardvreck Castle you can see the remains of a grand mansion. This was Edderchalder, or Calda House, which was built around 1720 by the up-and-coming Mackenzie family. Legend says that the woman who lived there was a witch who had cursed the district in a fit of rage, so that crops failed. Around 1737, after another miserable harvest, the curse was lifted when the house was struck by a lightning bolt.

INVERPOLLY

North of Ullapool the habitation is sparse and the landscape becomes altogether bigger and wilder, with giant, bare mountains looming out of bleak, bitter moorland.

The Inverpolly National Nature Reserve, managed by Scottish Natural Heritage, offers access to this fine, dramatic countryside in all its glory, and the visitor centre at Knockan is a good place to start. The diversity of habitats in the region is revealed, including bogs, lochs and patches of ancient woodland, with a corresponding diversity of flora.

A geology trail here illuminates the formation of the Assynt area, and part of the 'Moine Thrust' can be seen in the rocks of Knockan Cliff. There are excellent views from the top of the mountains of Coigach. Of these, Stac Pollaidh (2,008 ft/612m) is the most popular, and a relatively easy walk leads up from the minor road by Loch Lurgainn. Look out for deer and birds of prey, and you may even see signs of wildcats in the area. To the north on a clear day you can see the familiar form of Suilven (2,402 ft/732m), but this peak is strictly for experienced mountaineers.

There is a further extensive nature reserve at Inchnadamph. From this point the road leads round the shores of Loch Assynt, past the rocky ruins of Ardvreck Castle. Beyond this place is the popular harbour of Lochinver (this links up with a narrow and very scenic road from Loch Lurgainn). Up the coast, just north of the hamlet of Clachtoll, the circular remains of a broch from the first century AD can be seen on the shoreline.

LOCH NESS

It would be difficult for anyone but the most hardened sceptic to gaze out over the waters of Loch Ness without just the small hope of seeing something which might be interpreted as a 'sighting'.

Mentioned in writing as long ago as the 7th century, when St Adamnan's Life of St Columba tells of the saint calming the creature down after an apparent attack on a monk, the Loch Ness Monster – or, familiarly, Nessie – has become the focus of the tourist industry here. Drumnadrochit is the main centre for this, offering the Original Loch Ness Visitor Centre with a large-screen cinema, exhibition and sonar scanning cruises, and the Official

Visit

THE CALEDONIAN CANAL

Canals revolutionised Britain's transport system in the early 19th century. By the time of Queen Victoria's accession, more than 2000 miles (3,219km) of waterways had been constructed. One of the greatest feats of engineering was the 60-mile-long (96km) Caledonian Canal constructed along the Great Glen by Thomas Telford, who took advantage of the lochs – Lochy, Oich and Ness – which account for about two-thirds of the route. The linking sections of canal have a total of 28 locks, including 'Neptune's Staircase', a series of eight locks at Banavie. Begun in 1803 and finally opened in 1822, the canal was originally constructed to provide a safe route for maritime traffic, which previously had to brave the hazardous seas around the north of Scotland, but the scenic route was soon appreciated by tourists too. By 1900 they were filling three steamboats a day, bound from Inverness to Fort Augustus, Fort William and Oban. Cruise ships still operate on the canal, and there is a visitor centre at Fort Augustus.

Loch Ness Monster Exhibition with audio-visuals and a 'life-size' model of Nessie. You can hire a cabin cruiser, or visit the ruined Urquhart Castle on the shores of the loch, from where most sightings have been made.

Monster or no, Loch Ness is breaqthtakingly beautiful and it contains more water than all the lakes and reservoirs in England and in Wales put together. The loch is 24 miles (38.6km) long, 1 mile (1.6km) wide and 750 feet (228.6m) deep, making it one of the largest bodies of fresh water in Europe. The loch forms a major part of the Thomas Telford's Caledonian Canal, which links the west coast with the Moray Firth, and follows the line of the dramatic Great Glen, cutting Scotland in two distinct halves. This spectacular geological fault has provided a way through the mountains for centuries of travellers and is tracked today by the modern-day A82, which runs between Fort William and Inverness.

MALLAIG

This small, busy fishing harbour, facing the Isle of Skye across the Sound of Sleat, stands at the end of the A830 from Fort William, more romantically known as the 'Road to the Isles'. The term comes from the cattle-droving days, before the railway arrived in 1901, but it holds the evocative promise of a special destination for today's travellers. It is also the last stop on the famous West Highland Line, and ferries from Mallaig can take you on to Skye, Rum, Eigg, Muck and Canna. The town has an aquarium dedicated to local species and the fishing industry of the town, and a heritage centre. The steam train Jacobite runs from Fort William to Mallaig, passing Morar on the way.

A couple of miles outside Mallaig, at Morar, the waters of Scotland's deepest freshwater loch tumble and cascade down a spectacular waterfall and into a beautiful sandy bay. One of the long, white-sand beaches along

227

Activity

WEST HIGHLAND LINE

Mallaig is the terminus of the West Highland Line, which is celebrated as one of Britain's most scenic railway routes. Its construction was no easy task – the peat bogs of Rannoch Moor were traversed with a floating bed of brushwood, beneath tons of ash and earth; the rocky heights of Glenfinnan and the deeply indented coastline had to be crossed. Contractor Robert MacAlpine pioneered the structural use of concrete, building the high viaducts which give such magnificent views. Sit on the left for the outward journey (reserve a seat at peak times).

provided the setting for the iconic film *Local Hero*. A leisurely drive southwards is enchanting, passing through mixed woodland, with fine views to the islands. Allow yourself plenty of time – it's a slow, winding road and mainly single track, so do take care, until you reach the little church above Lochailort.

This part of the west coast has many associations with Prince Charles Edward Stuart. It was at Loch Nan Uamh, south of Arisaig, that the Prince landed in 1745 to raise an army, and it was from here that he left for France after his bitter defeat at Culloden the following year, leaving in his wake a strong tide of government retribution against the Highlanders.

SHIELDAIG & TORRIDON

The villages around Loch Torridon are picturesque, but cannot compete with the grandeur of some of the finest mountain scenery in Scotland. The road east from Shieldaig, a whitewashed, 18th-century village overlooking the pine-clad Shieldaig Island, gives views over Upper Loch Torridon to the huge mountain mass dominated by what Queen Victoria called 'that extraordinary mountain, Ben Liathach.'

Of red Torridonian sandstone, 750 million years old and 3,339 feet (1,024m) high, Liathach has a row

SHIELDAIG

SKYE

of seven peaks topped with shining white quartzite from 150 million years later. It forms part of the National Trust for Scotland's 16,100-acre (6,520ha) Torridon Estate. The Trust's Countryside Centre in Torridon village can advise on the best routes in the mountains, but guided walks are recommended if you want to tackle the 5-mile (8km) ridge between Liathach's peaks. The Deer Museum nearby has a herd of wild deer, and information about their life on the hills.

Further on, Beinn Eighe presents a forbidding face to the traveller, but like the other mountains has impressive corries to the north. Britain's first National Nature Reserve was founded here in 1951 to protect the native Caledonian pine forest on its slopes.

The road north of Loch Torridon, with wonderful views over to the Applecross peninsula, passes through Fasag, built to house families displaced in the clearances, and through several crofting settlements to end at Lower Diabaig, from where you can walk to Redpoint, far out on the coast of Wester Ross.

SKYE, ISLE OF

Skye is the largest and most famous of the Inner Hebrides, dominated from every view by the high peaks of the Cuillins. The jagged gabbro (igneous rock, like basalt) of the Black Cuillins and the pink, scree-covered granite of the Red Cuillins have proved an irresistible challenge for mountaineers, and the most inaccessible peaks were only conquered at the end of the last century. To the north on the Trotternish peninsula is an extraordinary broken ridge from which peaks and pillars loom eerily on a misty day.

Road signs written in Gaelic as well as English quickly tell you that you're in a different culture, and Skye retains a strong Gaelic identity, encouraged at the college, Sabhal Mòr Ostaig, in Sleat. At the Aros

231

Centre, just south of Portree, a forest walk illustrates the letters of the Gaelic alphabet. There are crofting museums at Colbost and Kilmuir, with reconstructed homesteads.

Portree is the island's capital, its colour-washed houses round the harbour, with fishing and pleasure vessels moored, are most attractive. This little town was named after a royal visit in 1540 by James V – port righ means king's harbour – and its formal square is a miniature delight. The town is the gateway to the Trotternish peninsula. Taking the road up the eastern side, look out for the distinctive column of the Old Man of Storr and other strange rock formations up on your left, and for the columnar formations and dramatic waterfall at the Kilt Rock on the coast to your right, just before Staffin. There are marvellous views from here across to the blue hills of the mainland.

Continuing around this peninsula you pass ruined Duntulm Castle and a memorial to Flora Macdonald, the Jacobite heroine who smuggled Prince Charles Edward Stuart here from his hiding place in South Uist in 1746. The Prince, disguised as 'Betty Burke', continued his escape to Raasay and then on to France. Flora was arrested and briefly imprisoned in the Tower of London. She later married a Skye man and emigrated to America; they returned to live down the coast at Kingsborough, and Flora's grave is there.

Heading west from Portree brings you to the wilder side of the island, with the Waternish and Duinish peninsulas like two long fingers reaching out towards the Outer Hebrides. At Carbost, the Talisker Distillery produces a distinctive peaty, smoky malt whisky. Dunvegan is the family seat of another powerful Skye clan, the MacLeods, and claims to be Scotland's oldest inhabited castle, occupied since the 13th century. Surrounded by a stout wall, and heavily restored and harled in the

STRATHPEFFER

mid-19th century, the castle is impressive if not beautiful – the treasures in its richly furnished rooms are well worth a look.

Broadford is the main centre for exploring the south of the island, and with its concentration of craftspeople, it is a good place to seek out good-quality souvenirs. The award-winning Serpentarium, run by experienced herpetologists, is well worth a visit. Here you can handle snakes, admire the lizards, frogs and tortoises, and learn more about their way of life.

If the weather is fine and clear, drive over to Elgol to experience some of Britain's most magnificent scenery. The road winds below the mighty Red Cuillins and beside Loch Slapin before descending an alarmingly steep road into Elgol (not suitable for caravans). You can see across to the island of Soay, with Canna, Rum and Eigg to the south. Try to make time for a boat trip, which offers a dramatic glimpse of Loch Coruisk.

After the barrenness of the mountains, Sleat seems a veritable Garden of Eden. The lovely Armadale Castle Gardens and the Museum of the Isles is well worth a visit. There are excellent exhibitions, genealogical research facilities, guided walks, a restaurant and much more. Look out for the special events held throughout the summer.

Skye is an unlikely crossroads among the islands. You can reach it by ferry from Mallaig (about 40 minutes), or across the strong currents by Glenelg (summer only), or across the new bridge at Kyle of Lochalsh. The bridge provoked controversy when it was built, but is low enough to be unobtrusive. Ferries to the outer islands leave from the harbour at Uig, on the Trotternish peninsula, and to Raasay from Sconser.

STRATHPEFFER

Once hailed as 'the Harrogate of the North', Strathpeffer is a curious phenomenon to find above the

Highland line – a genteel spa town, complete with Victorian architectural twirls such as verandahs and ornamental barge-boards.

Locals had known about the curative properties of the mineral springs here for centuries, but thanks to a serious scientific analysis of the water in 1819, Strathpeffer became a boom town. The first pump room opened the following year, and visitors flocked to fill the new hotels and villas. While never perhaps in the same league as Bath in Somerset, the town did attract some royal visitors from overseas, and the railway had to be specially extended from Dingwall to cater for the number of people drawn here. At the height of its fame there were even through-trains from London, though trains no longer come here.

Inevitably, tastes change, and Strathpeffer's popularity declined after World War II. Many of the spa buildings have disappeared, and the old wooden railway station now houses a museum of childhood. The Pump Room has been restored and offers interpretative displays covering the history of the spa. The town offers excellent golfing and recreational facilities. Don't miss the Pictish stone slab, set in a field near the station. Deeply carved with an inverted, patterned horseshoe shape above a standing eagle, its original purpose is unknown.

There are several good walks here, including the ridge of Knock Farril to the south, and through the woods to the Falls of Rogie to the west. Salmon may be seen in the Blackwater River here, and there are picnic sites between the trees.

ULLAPOOL

As you approach on the A835, the little whitewashed town of Ullapool is neatly laid out before you on a spit of land curving into Loch Broom. The tidy grid-plan of the streets reveals that this is a model town laid out to a plan developed by the British Fishery Society in 1788.

The site was chosen to provide a good fishing harbour, and to squeeze out the Dutch herring vessels which had taken advantage of the lack of local boats. The herring did not last, however, and, without the lifeline of the railway, the settlement declined.

The Fishery Society had chosen their site well, however, and in the first half of the 20th century boats came over from the east coast and fortunes revived. Until the mid-1990s, the local economy was given a boost by the 'Klondyker' factory ships from Eastern Europe, processing the catches of east coast trawlermen in the loch's sheltered waters. The collapse of the Russian economy saw them disappear and now tourism is the main industry. Learn more about crofting, fishing and emigration at Ulapool's small museum, set in a former church.

Ullapool is the gateway to the remote northwestern tip of Scotland, as well as the main ferry port for Stornoway, in the Outer Hebrides. Around the coast at Achiltibuie is the

Visit

OTTERS

Many people hope to see otters around the shores and lochs of Scotland, and, given a bit of luck, a pair of binoculars and some local guidance, there is every chance you will. The Kylerhea Otter Sanctuary on Skye is a good place to learn more about these shy creatures, and to seek advice on where and when to look. Loch Sunart on the southern coast of the Ardnamurchan peninsula, Loch Spelve in Mull and Loch Eynort in South Uist are places where you may see them. The Bright Water Visitor Centre at Kyleakin also has information about otters, and a museum to *Ring of Bright Water* author, Gavin Maxwell.

Hydroponicum, a scientific delight, where bananas and other exotic plants thrive without soil – seeing is believing! At the head of Loch Broom, take time out to stop and see the dramatic Corrieshalloch Gorge, and the suspension bridge just below the Falls of Measach.

ULLAPOOL

SKYE & NORTHERN HIGHLANDS

PLACES OF INTEREST

Aonach Mòr Gondola Ride
Torlundy.
Tel: 01397 705825;
www.nevis-range.co.uk

Armadale Castle Gardens and Museum of the Isles
Armadale, Sleat, Skye.
Tel: 01471 844305;
www.clandonald.com

Aros
Viewfield Road, Portree, Skye.
Tel: 01478 613649;
www.aros.co.uk

Beinn Eighe Visitor Centre
Aultroy.
Tel: 01445 760254

Black Isle Brewery
Old Allengrange, Munlochy, off A9.
Tel: 01463 811871;
www.blackislebrewery.com

Caledonian Canal Visitor Centre
Ardchattan House, Fort Augustus.
Tel: 01320 366493;
www.waterscape.com

Colbost Croft Museum
Colbost, by Dunvegan, Skye.
Tel: 01470 521296

Corrieshalloch Gorge National Nature Reserve
Braemore. Tel: 01445 781200
Open access.

Cromarty Courthouse Museum
Cromarty. Tel: 01381 600418;
www.cromarty-courthouse.org.uk

Dunvegan Castle
Skye. Tel: 01470 521206;
www.dunvegancastle.com

Eilean Donan Castle
Loch Duich, Kintail.
Tel: 01599 555202;
www.eileandonancastle.com

Fortrose Cathedral
Cathedral Square, Fortrose.
Tel: 01667 460232
Open access.

Gairloch Heritage Museum
Achtercairn, Gairloch.
www.gairlochheritagemuseum.org.uk

Glenfinnan Monument
Glenfinnan.
Tel: 01397 722250

Groam House Museum
High Street, Rosemarkie.
Tel: 01381 620961

240

Highland Wineries
Moniack Castle, Kirkhill.
Tel: 01463 831283;
www.moniackcastle.co.uk

Hugh Miller's House
Church Street, Cromarty.
Tel: 01381 600245

Hydroponicum
Achiltibuie, north of Ullapool.
Tel: 01854 622202;
www.thehydroponicum.com

Inverewe Garden
Poolewe.
Tel: 01445 781200

Inverness Museum & Art Gallery
Castle Wynd, Inverness.
Tel:01463 237114;
www.invernessmuseum.com

Knockan Visitor Centre
Inverpolly National Nature Reserve, off
A835 north of Ullapool.
Tel: 01854 613418

**Loch Ness 2000: Official Loch Ness
Monster Exhibition Centre**
Drumnadrochit.
Tel: 01456 450573;
www.loch-ness-scotland.com

Mallaig Heritage Centre
Tel: 01687 462085;
www.mallaigheritage.org.uk

Original Loch Ness Visitor Centre
Drumnadrochit.
Tel: 01456 450342;
www.lochness-centre.com

St Andrews Cathedral
15 Ardross Street, Inverness.
Tel: 01463 233535

Skye Museum of Island Life
Kilmuir, north of Uig, Skye.
Tel: 01470 552206

Talisker Distillery
Carbost, Skye.
Tel: 01478 614308;
www.malts.com

**Torridon Visitor Centre & Deer
Museum**
The Mains, Achnasheen.
Tel: 01445 791368

Treasures of the Earth
Corpach, by Fort William.
Tel: 01397 772283

Ullapool Museum
7–8 West Argyle Street, Ullapool.
Tel: 01854 612987;
www.ullapoolmuseum.co.uk

Urquhart Castle
Drumnadrochit, Loch Ness.
Tel: 01456 450551
West Highland Museum
Cameron Square, Fort William.
Tel: 01397 702169;
www.westhighlandmuseum.org.uk

FOR CHILDREN
Black Isle Wildlife Park
Drumsmittal, North Kessock.
Tel: 01463 731656
Bright Water Visitor Centre
The Pier, Kyleakin, Skye.
Tel: 01599 530040;
www.eileanban.org
Highland Museum of Childhood
The Old Station, Strathpeffer.
Tel: 01997 421031;
www.highlandmuseumofchildhood.org
Jacobite Steam Train
Operates between Fort William and
Mallaig.
Tel: 01524 737751
Follow the West Highland Line on
Harry Potter's Hogwarts steam train.
Kylerhea Otter Haven
Kylerhea, Skye.

Marine World
The Harbour, Mallaig.
Tel: 01687 462292
Skye Serpentarium/Reptile World
The Old Mill, Harrapool, Broadford,
Skye.Tel: 01471 822209;
www.skyeserpentarium.org.uk
Toy Museum
Holmisdale House, Glendale, Skye.
Tel: 01470 511240;
www.toy-museum.co.uk

SHOPPING
Castle Gallery
43 Castle Street, Inverness.
Tel: 01463 729512;
www.castlegallery.co.uk
Modern art.
Hebridean Jewellery
95 High Street, Fort William.
Tel: 01397 702033;
www.hebridean-jewellery.co.uk.
Jewellery in Celtic designs.
**Hector Russell Scottish Kiltmaker
Visitor Centre**
4–9 Huntly Street, Inverness.
Tel: 0800 980 4010;
www.hector-russell.com

Highland Stoneware
North Road, Ullapool.
Tel: 01854 612980;
www.highlandstoneware.com
Holm Mills Shopping
Village
Dores Road, Inverness.
Tel: 01463 223311
Weaving exhibitions.
Inverness Farmers' Market
Eastgate Precinct, Inverness.
Tel: 01309 651206
Nevisport
High Street, Fort William
Tel: 01397 704921; www.nevisport.com
Outdoor adventure sports equipment
and clothing.
Skye Batiks
The Green, Portree, Skye.
Tel: 01478 613331;
www.skyebatiks.com
Spean Bridge Mill
Spean Bridge, 10 miles (16km) north of
Fort William.
Tel: 01397 712260
Weaving mill.

SPORTS & ACTIVITIES
ADVENTURE SPORTS
Monster Activities
Great Glen Water Park, South Laggan,
by Spean Bridge.
Tel: 01809 501340;
www.monsteractivities.com
Abseiling and archery to kayaking,
windsurfing.
Raasay Outdoor Centre
Raasay House, Raasay, off north Skye.
Tel: 01478 660266;
www. raasayoutdoorcentre.co.uk
Sailing, cycling, climbing, kayaking and
more.
Whitewave: Skye's Outdoor Centre
Kilmuir, Skye.
Tel: 01470 542414;
www.white-wave.co.uk
Rock climbing, kayaking, guided walks
and more.
BOAT TRIPS
Bella Jane Boat Trips
Elgol, Skye. Tel: 0800 731 3089;
www.bellajane.co.uk
Explore Loch Coruisk, the Small Isles
and Skye wildlife. Advance booking
essential.

243

Calum's Seal Trips
Shore Front, Plockton.
Tel: 01599 544306;
www.calums-sealtrips.com

Cruise Loch Ness
Knockburnie, Inchnacardoch,
Fort Augustus.
Tel: 01320 366277;
www.cruiselochness.com

Dolphin Ecosse
Cromarty. Tel: 01381 600323

Jacobite Cruises
Tomnahurich Bridge, Glenurquhart
Road, Inverness.
Tel: 01463 233999; www.jacobite.co.uk

Inverness Dolphin Cruises
Shore Street Quy, Inverness.
Tel: 01463717900;
www.inverness-dolphin-cruises.co.uk

Seaprobe Atlantis
Kyle of Lochalsh.
Tel: 0800 980 4846;
www.seaprobeatlantis.com

Summer Isles cruises
From Ullapool:
Tel: 01853 612472
From Achiltibuie:
Tel: 01854 622315

CYCLING
Barneys
35 Castle Street, Inverness.
Tel: 01463 232249;
www.eastgatebackpackers.com

Highland Cycles
16A Telford Street, Inverness
Tel: 01463 234789;
www.highlandcycles.co.uk

Island Cycles
The Green, Portree, Skye.
Tel: 01478 613121; www.isbuc.co.uk
Cycle hire as well as fishing tackle hire.

Isle of Skye Golf Club
Sconser, Skye.
Tel: 01478 650414;
www.isleofskyegolfclub.co.uk
9-hole course.

Loch Ness Golf Course
Fairways, Castle Heather, Inverness.
Tel: 01463 713335
9- and 18-hole courses; also leisure
complex.

Strathypeffer Spa Golf Club
Golf Course Road, Strathpeffer.
Tel: 01997 421219;
www.strathpeffergolf.co.uk

LONG DISTANCE PATHS
Great Glen Way
Fort William to Inverness walking trail,
then cycle trail.
www.greatglenway.com

GOLF
Fort Augustus Golf Club
Markethill, Fort Augustus.
Tel: 01320 366660
Inverness Golf Club
Culcabock Road, Inverness.
Tel: 01463 239882;
www.invernessgolfclub.co.uk

HORSE-RIDING
Highland Riding Centre
Borlum Farm, Drumnadrochit.
Tel: 01456 450220; www.borlum.com
Highland Trekking and Trail Riding
Cougie, Tomich, Cannich.
Tel: 01456 415323; www.cougie.com
Pony trekking and trail riding.
Skye Riding Centre
Suledale, by Portree, Skye.
Tel: 01470 582419;
www.skyeridingcentre.co.uk
Pony trekking for all abilities, plus
disabled facilities.

GUIDED WALKS
Lochend Llama Treks
Invershiel, Glenshiel, by Kyle of
Lochalsh.
Tel: 07887 828756;
www.highlandllamatreks.com
Guided walks for all ability levels
– llamas carry the picnic lunch.

WINTER SPORTS
Nevis Range
Torlundy, north of Fort William.
Tel: 01397 705825;
www.nevis-range.co.uk
Ski and snowboarding centre for all
abilities.

ANNUAL EVENTS & CUSTOMS
Armadale
Skye Festival, late Jul, early Aug.
Inverness
Tattoo, Northern Meeting Park,
late Jul.
Plockton
Regatta, late Jul, early Aug.
Portree
Skye Highland Games, Aug.

The Ceilidh Place

14 West Argyle Street, Ullapool,
Highland, IV26 2TY
Tel: 01854 612103

An Ullapool institution since it opened
in 1970, this unique complex combines
an all-day coffee shop, a bar and a
restaurant with a bookshop, art gallery
and performance venue. Freshly
baked cakes are part of the appeal of
the all-day menu, but for something
more substantial you might try the
fennel, courgette and tomato gratin, or
perhaps a dish of locally caught fish.
Dogs are permitted in the garden.

Inverlochy Castle Hotel

Torlundy, by Fort William,
Highland, PH33 6SN
Tel: 01397 702177
www.inverlochycastlehotel.com

For a memorable Scottish afternoon
tea with a stunning backdrop of a loch
and high mountains, it would be hard
to beat this luxurious castle hotel just
north of Fort William. There's a wide
variety of teas on offer to accompany
the tempting array of scones, cakes,
pastries and biscuits, served in the
majestic Great Hall or the drawing
room which overlooks the loch.

Loch Torridon Country House Hotel

Torridon, Highland, IV22 2EY
Tel: 01445 791242

How do you fancy a real high tea? All
the silverware and best china, the tea
or coffee freshly brewed to accompany
the cucumber sandwiches, scones with
jam and cream and home-made cakes
– but taken on top of a mountain, and
led by a guide? It's one of the options
at this lovely hotel on the shore of Loch
Torridon. You can have it all at sea
level too, or opt for coffee and fresh
shortbread and enjoy the views.

TORRIDON

Applecross Inn
Shore Street, Applecross,
Highland, IV54 8LR
Tel: 01520 744262
Overlooking Skye and the Cuillins, this
lovely traditional white-painted inn
standing on the shore of the remote
and lovely Applecross peninsula is
known for its imaginative menu.
Local fish and game appear on the
menu, but it's the seafood that is
usually outstanding, from the simplest
prawn tails with Marie-Rose dip, to
king scallops cooked in garlic butter
with lemon, herbs and crispy bacon.
Puddings are tempting too, with fruit
crumble or raspberry cranachan.

The Old Inn
Carbost, Isle of Skye, IV47 8SR
Tel: 01478 640205
Stone walls and wooden floors
characterise this former croft house,
now an inn favoured by walkers
and climbers. At one time rents
were collected here. Now it serves
traditional and hearty Scottish food,
such as sausage hotpot, haggis and
neeps, and baked salmon. The patio
terrace overlooks Loch Hariport.

Plockton Inn and Seafood Restaurant
Innes Street, Plockton,
Highland, IV52 8TW
Tel: 01599 544222
www.plocktoninn.co.uk
Lying at the heart of pretty Plockton,
this former manse is the relaxed and
friendly setting for excellent food,
whether you're looking for deep fried
squid and grilled local sprats, or maybe
pheasant with a whisky and mustard
sauce. A smoke-house built behind
the hotel adds to the variety of flavours
on offer, and there are two gardens to
enjoy in summer, or blazing open fires
in winter.

SCOTLAND TOURIST INFORMATION

VisitScotland
PO Box 121, Livingston EH54 8AF.
Tel: 0845 2255121;
www.visitscotland.com

Edinburgh & Scotland
Information Centre
3 Princes Street, Edinburgh.
Tel: 0845 2255 121

Trossachs Discovery Centre &
Aberfoyle Tourist Information Centre
Main Street, Aberfoyle.
Tel: 08707 200604

Inveraray
Front Street, Inveraray.
Tel: 08707 200616;
www.visitscotlandheartlands.com

Oban
Argyll Square, Oban.
Tel: 01631 563122;
www.scotland-info.co.uk

OTHER INFORMATION

Historic Scotland
Longmore House, Salisbury Place,
Edinburgh EH9 1SH.
Tel: 0131 668 8800;
www.historic-scotland.gov.uk

National Trust for Scotland
Wemyss House, 28 Charlotte Square,
Edinburgh EH2 4ET.
Tel: 0131 243 9300;
www.scotlandforyou.co.uk

Scottish Natural Heritage
12 Hope Terrace, Edinburgh EH9 2AS.
Tel: 0131 447 4784;
www.snh.org.uk

Scottish Wildlife Trust
Cramond House, 16 Cramond Glebe
Road, Edinburgh EH4 6NS.
Tel: 01131 312 7765; www.swt.org.uk

Royal Society for the
Protection of Birds
Dunedin House, 25 Ravelston Terrace,
Edinburgh EH4 3TP.
Tel: 0131 311 6500;
www.rspb.org.uk

FORESTRY COMMISSION SCOTLAND

Silvan House, 231 Corstorphine Road, Edinburgh EH12 7AT.
Tel: 0845 367 3787;
www.forestry.gov.uk/scotland

Cairngorms National Park Authority
Tel: 01479 873535;
www.cairngorms.co.uk

Traveline
Tel: 0870 608 2608;
www.traveline.org.uk
For public transport inquiries.

Caledonian MacBrayne (Calmac)
Tel: 0870 565 0000;
www.calmac.co.uk
Main inter-island ferry operator.

Glenelg Ferry
Tel: 01599 511302;
www.skyeferry.co.uk

Royal Mail Postbusservice
Tel: 08457 740740;
www.postbus.royalmail.com
Operates to inacccessible rural communities.

National Rail Enquiry Service
Tel: 08457 484950;
www.nationalrail.co.uk
For all train enquiries.

First ScotRail
Tel: 08457 550033;
www.firstscotrail.com
Main rail services operator within Scotland; includes West Highland Line.

Scottish Citylink
Tel: 0870 550 5050;
www.citylink.co.uk
Main inter-city coach services across Scotland.

Weather
www.onlineweather.com

INDEX

Page numbers in **bold** refer to main entries

A
Aberfeldy 65, 66, **67-8**
Aberfoyle 89
Aberlour 183
Abernethy Forest 164-9
Achnabreck 128
Achrey Forest 2-3
Adam's Grave 117
Affric, Loch 205-6
Aidan 132
Albany, Robert Stewart, Duke of 73
Albert, Prince 112, 169
Alexander II, King 180
Anstruther 34
Applecross **202**, 231
Ardmeanach peninsula 137
Ardnamurchan **107**
Argyll, Dukes of 46, 124-8
Arran, Isle of **108-11**, 133
Arthur's Seat 32, 40, 44
Atholl, Dukes of 79, 80, 88
Aviemore 156, 159, 162, **163-4**, 183, 192
Awe, Loch 104, 128, 135, 151

B
Ballater 170
Balloch 89, 135
Balmaha 136
Balmoral 166-7, 169, 170, 173
Bannockburn, Battle of 50

Barrie, J M 82
Beinn Eighe 231
Ben Cruachan 135, **136**
Ben Lawers 68, 81
Ben Liathach 228-31
Ben Macdhui **209**
Ben Nevis 196, 206-7, **209**
Bidean nam Bian 15
Black Isle **202-4**
Blair Castle 88
Boat of Garten **164-9**
Braan, River 63, 80
Braemar 168, **169-70**
brochs 215, **216**
Brodick 108, 109
Bronze Age 111
Burns, Robert 67, 112
Bute 117

C
Cairnbaan 104
Cairngorm Mountains 10, 81-2, 156, 160, **170-5**, 183, 191
Calda House **224**
Caledonian Canal 200, **225**, 227
Caledonian MacBrayne **142**
Calgary 137
Callander **68-73**
Campbell clan 80-1, 121, 128
Campbeltown 132, 133
Cannich **205**, 247
Central Highlands 154-93
Charlie, Bonnie Prince 67-8, 88, 176, 216-19, 228, 232
Civil War 117

Clava Cairns **184**
Clootie Dumpling **169**
Columba, St 80, 132-3, 138, 221, 227
Comrie **73**
coopers **183**
Cowal Bird Gardens 117
Craigellachie Bridge 159
Crail 34, 37
Crathes Castle 159
Crieff 63, 65, 70-1, **73-5**
Crinan Canal 104, **112**, 113, 133
Cromarty 204, 205
Cuillins 231, 235
Culloden, Battle of 160, **176**, 219, 228

D
Dalriada **132**
Deeside 156-7, **169-70**, 173
Discovery, R R S 65, 76
Dochart, Falls of 19
Dog Falls 15
dolphins **205**
Doune 72, 73
Drummond Castle 74, 75
The Drummonds, Crieff 70-1
Duart Castle 137
Dulnain Bridge 169
Duncan, King 138, 221
Dundee 60-1, **76-9**
Dunkeld 63, **79-80**
Dunmore Park 50
Dunoon **112-17**

E
Earn, Loch 75
East Neuk villages **34–7**, 56
Edinburgh 28–9, 32, 36, **37–45**
Edward I, King 50
Edward II, King 50
Edzell Castle 63
Eilean Donan Castle **202**, 203
Elie 34, 37
Elizabeth, Queen Mother 82

F
Falls of Dochart 19
ferries **142**
Fife 28, 34–7, **45–9**
Fife Coastal Path 34
Fillan, St 34
Fingal's Cave 138
Forres **176–80**
Fort Augustus 200
Fort William 136, 208, **205–12**, 221, 227
Forth, Firth of 37, 40, 50
Fortingall **67**, 68
Fortrose 204
Fyne, Loch 112, 124

G
Gairloch 210–11, **212–15**
Garten, Loch 164
Glamis Castle 82–5
Glasgow 17, 89, 100, 105, **118–21**, 135
Glen Affric 15, 205–6

Glen Coe 100–1, 103, 120, **121–4**, 136
Glen Falloch 55
Glen Lyon 68
Glen Roy 212
Glenelg 214, **215–16**
Glenfinnan 200, **216–19**
Glenfinnan Viaduct 17, **221**
Glens of Angus 81–2
Gow, Neil 80
Grampian Mountains 81
Grantown-on-Spey 183–4
Great Glen 196, 209, 220, 225, 227
Greyfriar's Bobby **44**

H
Hamilton, Dukes of 108
Hebrides 15, **231–5**, 237
The Hermitage, Dunkeld 63
Highland Boundary 73, 108
Highlands 8, 10, 58–97, 98–153, 154–93, 194–251
Holy Loch 117
Holyrood Palace 40
Hooker, Joseph 133

I
Inchcailloch 136
Inchmahone Priory 72
Inverary 17, 20, **124–8**, 141
Inverewe Garden 196, 199, 218, **219–20**
Inverness 199, 204, **220–1**, 227
Inverpolly **224–5**

Iona 100, **137–8**
Iron Age 68, 104, 216, 224

J
Jacobites 79, 88, 160, 170, 176, 181, 209, 216–19, 221, 232
James II, King 34, 49
James IV, King 49, 72, 107
James V, King 232
James VI, King 40, 49
Jura, Isle of 142

K
Katrine, Loch 87, 89
Kenneth MacAlpin 80
Kilchurn Castle 104, 151
Killiecrankie 88, 96
Killin 19, **80–1**, 89
Kilmartin 100, **128–32**
Kilmory Castle 133
Kingussie 160, **180–1**
Kinloch Castle 199
Kintyre **132–3**
Kirriemuir **81–5**
The Knock, Crieff 63
Kyles of Bute 117

L
Laggan 184
language **111**
Loch an Eilean 164
Loch Ness **225–7**
Loch of the Lowes 79
Lochgilphead **133–5**

253

Lomond, Loch 10, 88–9, 103, 130–1, 134, **135–7**, 152
Lorimer, Robert 49
Luma Light Factory, Glasgow 105
Luss 135–6
Lyon, River 68

M
MacAlpine, Robert 221
Macbeth 138, 176
MacCaig 141
Macdonald, Flora 142, 221, 232
Macdonald clan 103, 121
McGonagall, William **75**
MacGregor, Rob Roy 68–72
Machrie Moor 111
Mackenzie, Sir Alexander 204–5
Mackenzie, Osgood 219–20
Mackenzie clan 202, 224
Mackintosh, Charles Rennie 17, 118–21
Macleod, George 107
Mallaig 200, 221, 226, **227–8**
Malt Whisky Trail 183
Maree, Loch 212, 215
Mary, Queen of Scots 49, 72, 86, 204
Mary II, Queen 121
Maxwell, Gavin 216, 237
Meigle 81
Mendelssohn, Felix 138
Menteith, Lake of 72
Moniack Castle **220**

Morar 228
Moray Firth 204, 205, 227
Morlich, Loch 164
Morvern **107**
Mount Stuart House, Bute 117
Mull 12–13, 103, 107, **137–9**
Mull of Kintyre 112, 133
Munros 15

N
Na Keal, Loch 103
National Trust for Scotland 49, 50, 79, 81, 124, 170, 204, 220, 228
Ness, Loch 23, 196–7, **225–7**
Nethy Bridge 169
Northern Highlands 194–251
Nuclear Command Centre **46**

O
Oban 15, 98, 140, **141–2**, 143
ospreys **79**, 164
otters **237**

P
'Parallel Roads' **212**
Perth 84, **85–6**
Pictish stones **81**
Pilate, Pontius **67**
The Pineapple **50**
Pitlochry 9, **86–8**
Pittenweem 31, 34
Pluscarden Abbey 178–9, 180
Portree 231–2

Q
Queen Elizabeth Forest Park 136

R
Rannoch Moor **121–4**, 221
reindeer **163**
Rennie, John 112
Rhum 199
Robert the Bruce 50, 86, **108**
Rothesay 117
Royal Botanic Garden, Edinburgh **37**
RSPB 164, 181
Ruthven Barracks 160, 181

S
St Andrews 28, 32, **45–9**
St Monans 34–7
Sandaig 216
Sanna Bay 107
Scone Palace 86
Scotland's Secret Bunker **46**
Scott, Robert Falcon 65, 82
Scott, Sir Walter 37, 89
Shakespeare, William 176, 221
Shiel, Loch 216, 221
Shieldaig **228**, 229
skiing **121**
Skye, Isle of 24, 200, 227, 230, **231–5**
Southern Highlands 58–97
Spanish Armada **141**
Spey, River 156, 159, 164, 183